LOSING MY MIND, FINDING GOD

D. L. Thomason

ISBN 9798234112392

Scripture Quotations

Unless otherwise indicated, most Scripture quotations are taken from the New American Standard Bible (NASB) and the New King James Version® (NKJV).

Additional translations, including the Berean Standard Bible (BSB), English Standard Version (ESV), Amplified Bible (AB), Berean Literal Bible (BLB), Holman Christian Standard Bible (HCSB), God's Word Translation (GWT), and Christian Standard Bible (CSB), are occasionally used to provide added clarity, nuance, emphasis, and deeper insight into the discussion and biblical text. These translations are noted accordingly.

Disclaimer

The information in this book is for educational and spiritual purposes only. It is based on the author's personal experiences and biblical study.

This work is not intended to be a substitute for professional medical advice, diagnosis, or treatment. Always seek the advice of your physician, licensed counselor, or another qualified health provider with any questions you may have regarding a medical or mental health condition.

Never disregard professional medical advice or delay seeking it because of something you have read in this book.

In Memoriam

This book is dedicated to the loving memory of my dad, Manuel Lynn Thomason, whose life continues to leave an enduring imprint upon my own, and to my son, Gryphon Pyrus Thomason, whom I never had the opportunity to hold in this life, yet will always carry in my heart.

Through faith in Jesus Christ and the promises of God, I hold firmly to the hope of Heaven. I look forward to the day we are joyfully reunited in His presence, where sorrow, pain, and separation will be no more.

Table of Contents

Introduction

I was diagnosed with depression at fifteen years old, and I spent my sixteenth birthday in a mental health facility. My brother had been admitted first. Sometime later, during a visit to see him, my parents left me there too. Needless to say, the experience left me carrying more than a diagnosis. Some trust issues lingered as well.

Now, over thirty years later, I look back and wonder: If I had taken my mental health more seriously, would I be in the same situation I am in now? Would greater understanding, counseling, or support during those years have better equipped me to navigate the challenges I would later face?

These questions are no longer a focus in my life. My parents had never been parents before, and they did the best they knew how to do. I love them for that. Today, I take each day as it comes and try to do the best I can with what I have been given. Some days are heavier than others, and some are more manageable.

What I have come to understand, however, is that one of my greatest struggles is feeling mentally limited and not being able to show up as the man I want to be for my family. They are gracious, patient, and loving toward me, yet I often feel that I fall short and let them down.

As a God-fearing man, I am called to lead my family toward Him in love. Yet I often struggle to lead myself and to remain loving every single day. My wife would often tell me, *"You aren't happy unless something bad is happening."* Over time, I came to realize that my emotional maturity was far lower than my physical age.

It is a strange thing to live with mental illness. On the surface, someone can look at you and assume you are healthy and functioning well. It may not be until later, after they have spent more time with you, that the relationship begins to crumble. This doesn't have to be a cold, hard fact, but in my personal experience, it has been a recurring pattern.

Mark Twain famously said, "Out of all the things I've lost, I miss my mind the most." Somewhere in the back of my thoughts, I still believe that one day everything will be okay. I'll wake up, my brain will work perfectly, my family will see the best version of me, and my relationships will no longer feel as strained as they do now.

"So also is the resurrection of the dead. The body is sown in corruption; it is raised in incorruption. It is sown in dishonor; it is raised in glory. It is sown in weakness; it is raised in power. It is sown a natural body; it is raised a spiritual body. There is a natural body, and there is a spiritual body" (1 Corinthians 15:42-44 NKJV).

I am God's masterpiece, a work in progress. With great hope and anticipation, I look forward to the things He has prepared to work in me, things immeasurably beyond my greatest imagination (Ephesians 3:20). He makes all things beautiful in His time (Ecclesiastes 3:11).

I hope this book encourages and helps you, or a loved one, on your journey along this path we call life.

Chapter 1
Alone

I didn't struggle with being alone. I struggled with *feeling* alone around everyone else.

Excitement and stress share similar physiological markers. So even when I was excited, I had tremendous trouble "*Feeling*" it. My body usually interpreted it as "*Stress*", which drove me inward and further away from seeking others out. Proximity to people, even loved ones, does not automatically mean you feel seen or heard. It is possible to feel alone, even when you are not.

"And He came out and went, as was His habit, to the Mount of Olives; and the disciples also followed Him. Now, when He arrived at the place, He said to them, 'Pray that you do not come into temptation.' And He withdrew from them about a stone's throw, and He knelt and began to pray" (Luke 22:39–41).

Do you suppose Jesus felt alone in the garden?

He was physically separate from His friends. He knew His betrayal was coming. He knew His companions would desert Him. He knew the agony, torture, and mockery He would suffer. This made Him sorrowful, grieved, and deeply troubled, even to the point of death. His flesh did not want to endure what He knew was coming.

Was Jesus truly alone? His apostles were nearby, about half a football field away, but they did not really understand what He was enduring or what He was about to face. They were close in proximity but far away in perception and empathy.

How do you feel when your friends or family don't truly understand what you are going through? I have had well-meaning people tell me that "You don't have it as bad as …", or "You don't need medicine." What do you think and tell yourself in moments like that?

When Jesus was in the garden, God, the Master Gardener and Father of all comfort, sent comfort to Him in the form of an angel (John 15:1; 2 Corinthians 1:3).

"Father, if You are willing, remove this cup from Me; yet not My will, but Yours be done. Now an angel from heaven appeared to Him, strengthening Him" (Luke 22:42–43). The word *angel* here literally means a messenger from God. Even though it appeared that Jesus was by Himself, He was not truly alone (John 16:32).

Many times, in the throes of deep depression, I would lie on my bed, immersed in a darkened shroud of thoughts, feeling hopeless and alone, even though my loving family was only a room or two away. Yet God was always right there, waiting for me to reach out to Him (Acts 17:27).

When you feel alone, lost, judged, sad, depressed, or as if your life may not amount to much, do you remember to seek God's will in those moments? Jesus chose to put God's will before His own and to listen to His Father's words rather than His own thoughts and emotional tugging. Will you allow your feeling of being alone to draw you closer to God (1 Timothy 5:5)?

Elijah

Let us look at another example from the Bible. In 1 Kings 18, Elijah, by God's might, overcame and defeated the prophets of Baal. Then he received an alarming message: "may the gods do to me and more so, if by about this time tomorrow I do not make your life like the life of one of them." And he was afraid and ran for his life. (1 Kings 19:2–3)

Elijah experienced a moment of triumph, only to be informed by the queen that she planned to have him killed. I do not know your situation, but I have never had to run for my life. I cannot fathom how terrifying and nerve-racking that must have been.

Verse 3 tells us that Elijah left his servant in Beersheba. "But he went himself a day's journey into the wilderness, and came and sat down under a broom tree" (verse 4). He then told God that it was enough, that he felt he had personally failed, and that he wished to die. Have you ever had feelings similar to Elijah's? Has all your effort and momentum seemed to fail? Have you ever seen no hope and no purpose in going on?

"Then he lay down and fell asleep under a broom tree; but behold, an angel was touching him, and he said to him, 'Arise, eat!'" (verse 5).

Elijah left his companion and traveled farther, just as Jesus had, and now he was mentally at the point of death. He seemed alone and felt doomed. And again, we see God sending comfort in the form of a messenger, an angel, to strengthen him.

Let us notice something important here. Verses 5–7 show us that Elijah was so depressed, anxious, and mentally taxed that all he could do was eat and sleep. Sometimes, when we feel alone, worn down, and helpless, the most we can do is respond the same way Elijah did.

"Arise, eat; because the journey is too long for you" (verse 7).

Elijah's current course of life was too much for him to manage. Sometimes our journey and path may seem too great for us as well. Chronic illness, the loss of a loved one, financial loss, peer pressure, having a child with special needs, feeling out of place at school or work, and many other burdens can leave us overwhelmed and unsure of the way forward.

And that is okay.

Life is not a sprint; it is a marathon, and we run one day at a time (Matthew 6:34) as God grants us life (Acts 17:25). He directs our steps (Psalm 119:133), and when we try to run ahead of Him, we get lost (2 John 9). Elijah was mentally lost because he relied only on appearances and failed to fully acknowledge God's perfect guiding power.

After resting, Elijah continued his journey and came to Horeb, the mountain of God. He found a cave and went in to spend the night. Then God told Elijah, "Go out and stand on the mountain" (1 Kings 19:11).

"And behold, the LORD was passing by! And a great and powerful wind was tearing out the mountains and breaking the rocks into pieces before the LORD; but the LORD was not in the wind. And after the wind, there was an earthquake, but the LORD was not in the earthquake. And after the earthquake, a fire, but the LORD was not in the fire; and after the fire, a gentle blowing" (verses 11–12).

To better understand this, let us look at the prior conversation between God and Elijah and consider it in light of what we have already discussed. "What are you doing here, Elijah?" (verse 9).

God fully knew all that had happened and everything that was going on with Elijah spiritually, physically, emotionally, and mentally. So why would God ask Elijah this question? Was the question for God to better understand the situation, or was it for Elijah to speak honestly with God and gain clarity for himself?

"I have been zealous for the LORD, the God of armies, for the sons of Israel have abandoned Your covenant, torn down Your altars, and killed Your prophets with the sword. And I alone am left, and they have sought to take my life" (verses 9-10).

Have you ever felt like you were finally getting ahead in life, whether spiritually, financially, relationally, physically, or mentally, only to seemingly take three steps backward? Don't worry. This is a normal part of the marathon.

God showed Elijah mighty, overwhelming forces of nature, and the Bible makes sure to tell us that God was not in them. If we look at the events in our lives that seem scary, threatening, and intense, and we allow them to keep us from moving forward, are we trusting more in those events or in the One who can control their outcome (Mark 4:39–41)?

God had called Elijah to get up and leave the cave, but Elijah did not. He stayed inside.

Then a sound of gentle blowing, or "a still small voice" in the NKJV, came. When Elijah heard it, he wrapped his face in his cloak, went out, and stood at the entrance of the cave (1 Kings 19:13).

God calls us to move and take action, but sometimes we hide in the shadows, waiting for life to pass us by until circumstances seem more favorable. He calls us to draw closer to Him in frightening moments, not just afterward. God invited Elijah to take a different posture in life than the one he had been carrying. Elijah had sat down and lain down, and now God called him to stand.

"'Not by might nor by power, but by My Spirit,' says the LORD of armies" (Zechariah 4:6).

Sometimes we miss God's gentle voice because we are only listening for the loud, destructive events in our lives, whether real or imagined. God's Word is powerful, active, and alive, and it can divide our thoughts and intentions (Hebrews 4:12). His words can guide and direct us when we feel lost and confused, if we let them.

We have to listen amid the noise.

What are you currently listening to in your life? Is it helping you, or is it hurting you?

A Valuable Key

When God asked Elijah what was going on, Elijah revealed an important piece of information: "I alone am left" (1 Kings 19:10). Elijah felt and believed that he was completely alone.

While we previously compared his setting to Jesus', there is a stark difference in the mindset of each man. Jesus said, "And He who has sent Me is with Me. He has not left Me alone" (John 8:29). Jesus knew beyond a doubt that God was with Him, even when His closest friends would fail Him and let Him down. Even when they all deserted Him and ran away, Jesus still knew who was in control of the storms of life.

When we face those storms, who do we put our faith in: God, the responses of others, or even ourselves? Do we try to bring everything under our control and force life to go the way we think it should? Or do we patiently do what we can and allow God to do His part?

God asked Elijah a clarifying question and then enlightened him. "I will leave 7,000 in Israel, all the knees that have not bowed to Baal" (1 Kings 19:18). God helped Elijah see a clearer picture beyond his own perception. When we see from God's perspective, we can realize that even when it seems we are alone, there are thousands on our side (1 Peter 2:9–10). God gave Elijah hope, purpose, and direction, and He can do the same for you.

It may not feel like it, and we may not see it immediately. It takes faith to believe that what God says is true. Don't stop looking for and seeking out meaningful connections. The reality is that people in your immediate circle may not truly understand what you are going through. Sometimes experience is the true teacher, and if they have not experienced it, they may not be able to fully understand it.

And that is okay.

That doesn't mean their words, thoughts, or actions are futile or insincere. It simply means there is room for growth, both yours and theirs. Where do you shut down around others? Where do you need to show compassion toward those who may not understand your situation?

The Hunter Stalks His Prey

An important truth to keep at the front of our minds is this: Satan wants us to feel alone and isolated. He is the Father of all lies (John 8:44), and we fall right into his trap when we lie to ourselves and believe that we are alone in this struggle. We are not ignorant of his devices, so we must be on high alert when we begin to feel separated and abandoned (2 Corinthians 2:11).

"It is **not good** for the man to be alone; I will make a helper suitable to Him" (Genesis 2:18). Here we see the beginning of marriage and a deeper insight into the fact that God designed us to be social beings. It is interesting to note that the word ALONE in Hebrew, when transliterated into English, is BAD. In this context: ALONE = BAD.

Think about nature and the animal world. Whether in pods, sounders, herds, schools, or flocks, many animals travel in groups. Why does this occur? It is by God's design. When animals are alone, they become vulnerable. When stalking, a hunter will single out a weak one to kill. The same is true of the lion who seeks to devour us, the devil (1 Peter 5:8). He wants us to believe a lie. He wants us to feel alone so he can separate us and destroy us spiritually.

This usually isn't a single event but a process we go through. "Blessed is the man who ***walks*** not in the counsel of the ungodly, nor ***stands*** in the path of sinners, nor ***sits*** in the seat of the scornful" (Psalm 1:1 NKJV). Elijah went through a similar process: walking, standing, and sitting.

Notice that the verse refers to the counsel of the *ungodly*. What guidance do we give ourselves? Is it God-inspired or fear-based?

God calls us to get up and move. And when we go forth in His might, we can walk and not faint, run and not grow weary, and mount up with wings like eagles (Isaiah 40:31). This is a spiritual reality, not a physical one. You will not instantly become a marathon runner, physically or spiritually, but you can work toward it.

This takes training, perseverance, and a strength beyond what we may currently possess. It is a strength that God supplies as He carries us forward (Deuteronomy 1:31). Our outward body may be perishing, but our inner being should be growing stronger each day in God's might (2 Corinthians 4:16). We are not merely bodies of flesh with souls. We are souls surrounded by human bodies, and we wage war spiritually from within. We interact and process through the body, but what we experience has a lasting impact internally (Romans 12:2).

Where might you be walking away from God's calling on your journey?

Where are you currently standing?

Where have you taken a seat and simply started watching life pass by?

God Sent An Angel

If you recall, in both Jesus' and Elijah's stories, God sent an angel to comfort them. Hebrews 1:14 tells us that angels are ministering spirits sent to serve God's people. I am not saying that each of us has a "guardian angel," I don't believe that is what the text implies. But we can take courage in knowing that God sees our path, sees our needs, and sends help our way. *"We were afflicted on every side: conflicts on the outside, fears inside. But God, who comforts the discouraged, comforted us by the arrival of Titus"* (2 Corinthians 7:5–6).

Remember, we said that an angel was a messenger sent by God. Hebrews speaks of spiritual messengers, but sometimes God sends comfort in the form of a physical messenger. Just as we may not see the path of the wind or know exactly how bones are formed in the womb, we won't always clearly see all the activity God is orchestrating in our lives (Ecclesiastes 11:5).

But rest assured, He sees you. He sees your activity. He knows your struggle. He knows how to help you, and He knows the best path for you.

One Thing

If you take away only one thing from this chapter, hold tightly to this: ***You are not alone***. You might feel alone, isolated, misunderstood, and overlooked at times, but you are not. Satan wants you to believe that lie so you can be picked off, hunted down, and led toward spiritual death. Only then can a person truly be separated from God's presence (2 Thessalonians 1:9).

God sends helpers into our lives. Look for them. Don't refuse to be comforted (Genesis 37:35). Sometimes we can be that "angel" in someone else's life.

Remember, there are countless others who understand what you are going through and are in a similar boat, even if those closest to you may not be. That is okay. Our mess often becomes our strongest message. The more you focus on helping others see that they are not truly alone, the more you may realize that God has it all under control and that He is watching over you and caring for you.

"I am not alone, because the Father is with me. These things I have spoken to you that you may have peace. In the world you will have tribulation, but take courage; I have overcome the world" (John 16:32–33).

Chapter 2

Mental Illness

When I was younger, I had no idea what "healthy" meant. I knew whether I was fat or skinny, but health was an elusive word that seemed beyond my grasp. And while I had no real awareness of the physical implications, I never would have dreamed that there was a mental side to that coin as well.

When you hear the words mental health, what emotions come to the surface? Do any specific instances or stories come to mind? What exactly is mental health?

Mental health is a person's emotional, psychological, and social well-being. It affects how people think, feel, act, and cope with life's stresses. The biblical truths in this book are meant to encourage spiritual understanding, growth, and healing for all. While the primary focus is mental illness, the well-being of those affected by autism, ADHD, neurodivergence, intellectual or developmental disabilities

(IDD), and those who are neurotypical is also taken into consideration.

According to the National Institute of Mental Health (NIMH), a mental illness, often temporary and treatable, refers to a diagnosable condition involving significant and enduring disruptions in a person's thinking, emotional state, mood, or behavior. This can cause significant distress and impair daily functioning, including in social, work, or family settings, often requiring professional care and treatment. In 2022, it was estimated that one in five U.S. adults lived with a mental illness.

Do you struggle with your own mental health? Do you have friends or family who do?

I wrote the original manuscript for this book in 2022, during the pandemic. According to data published by Mental Health America, "We are seeing the highest levels of anxiety and depression since the pandemic hit the U.S. This is a troubling trend fueled by *loneliness* and *isolation*." These are two ideas previously discussed in chapter 1.

There is no doubt that we are seeing increases in mental illness, as well as greater awareness and more available treatments. The question I would like to pose is this: *What does the Bible say about mental illness?*

This is clearly an important issue. If God's Word contains "everything that pertains to life and godliness" (2 Peter 1:3), then surely there must be something in it about mental health, right? Yet, if you search online for information about mental illness and the Bible, you may find that there are not many Scriptures that address this topic directly. There are certainly none that specifically mention bipolar disorder, schizophrenia, or social anxiety disorder. So how is a Christian supposed to receive spiritual guidance on these matters?

When my brother and I were kids, we had an outside dog named Spike. He had a little house in the backyard, along with his own water bowl and food dish. One day, we noticed that the neighbor's dog had been coming over and eating our pup's food. The neighbor was informed, yet his dog kept consuming the food day after day. How is a person supposed to receive spiritual guidance for a problem like that?

In a similar way, we can receive spiritual guidance concerning mental illness. The Bible may not distinctly address every specific issue, but God teaches us indirectly how to be direct. He uses principles, stories, examples, and warnings to teach profound truths that foster deeper relational understanding, enabling us to walk wisely in our lives. Let us look at some examples of mental illness in the Old Testament.

In Deuteronomy 28:1–14, we see God listing the blessings the nation of Israel would receive if they diligently followed His voice and commands. From verse 15 to the end of the chapter, we see the curses that would come upon them for not listening and obeying. "I will strike you with insanity, blindness, and with confusion of mind" (verse 28).

He does not give the same curses today (Hebrews 8:13), but apart from His perfect presence, illness and suffering have come into view.

In the beginning, when God created, He pronounced it *good.* After man was formed, God said it was *very good* (Genesis 1:25, 31). Sin separates mankind from God (Romans 5:18), and part of the resulting collapse was mental illness. From the point of humanity's fall, a slow process of decay began. This affects not only the world around us (Isaiah 51:6) but also the integrity of the human genome.

There are now over 6,000 known genetic disorders in human beings. I am not claiming that genetics is the cause of all mental illness, or that a personal lack of faith is either. Inherited traits, chemical imbalances, life trauma, ongoing stress, and social factors such as poverty or isolation can all contribute to mental illness. However, the state of mental health today suggests that the perfect specimen once seen in the garden, in Adam and Eve, is no longer present.

Let's examine some of the words used in Deuteronomy 28:28. According to Strong's Concordance, the word *Insanity* (7697) in Hebrew means "madness" or "craziness." We are familiar with the word *crazy*, which can refer to being of unsound mind or out of control. Looking at this simple definition, we can all seem "crazy" at times. Another definition of "*insane*," from Wiktionary, is "unable to think clearly or sensibly." Yet again, this can describe anyone at a given moment, because we all become frustrated and flustered on occasion.

Deuteronomy also mentions *confusion of mind*, which is something every human on this planet can experience. On any typical Tuesday, a person may seem "crazy," "insane," or "confused" according to these definitions. So what does all of this mean? Let's look at another biblical example to gain some understanding.

In 1 Samuel 21, David is fleeing from Saul's presence. Here is another story in which a man fears for his life and appears to be alone (1 Samuel 21:1, 10). David went to Achish, the king of Gath, and became greatly afraid of him.

"So he changed his behavior before them, pretended madness in their hands, scratched at the doors of the gate, and let saliva fall on his beard. Then Achish said to his servants, 'Look, this man is insane. Why have you brought him to me?'" (verses 13–14 NKJV).

This passage is very interesting because it explains what madness, or insanity, looked like thousands of years ago in their time. Not only does it describe it, but the passage also continues as though they were fully aware of it and had a working knowledge of this mental illness and its characteristics.

Earlier, I mentioned that mental health awareness is growing. So why does everyone not already know about it today? The underlying nature of mental illness remains biologically and psychologically consistent, but diagnosis, prevalence rates, societal definitions, and treatments have evolved dramatically over time. With modern medicine and our ability to communicate, things have changed greatly since David's day, and even more so since Adam's time in the garden. The farther we move from perfection, the more aware we become of imperfection.

In Luke 8, Jesus encounters a man who was mad and of unsound mind, a man who had been struggling with inner demons for a long time (verse 27). Jesus cast the demons out. Notice what the text says: "Then they went out to see what had happened, and came to Jesus, and found the man from whom the demons had departed, sitting at the feet of Jesus, clothed and in his *right mind*" (verse 35).

I am not claiming that demon possession occurs today, but many people have their own "demons" that they struggle with. Mental illness is one I have fought my entire adult life. "God has not given us a spirit of fear, but of power and love and of a *sound mind*" (2 Timothy 1:7 NKJV).

This does not mean you will be instantly cured of your mental struggles. But it does mean that as you sit at Jesus' feet, as the possessed man did, and grow by listening to and following His words, the right ways of thinking, understanding, and speaking will be made available to you (1 Corinthians 13:11). As we learn to follow God's will in the face of our own storms, intense feelings, and mental warfare, we will be filled with the mind of Christ (Philippians 2:5).

The people in that area knew who the possessed man was and what his life had looked like. He had lived in tombs. He had gone around naked. Chains and shackles couldn't hold him. No one could travel that way because of how violent he was. Yet now that he was in his right mind, *they were afraid.*

As in Elijah's story, God was not in the scary, destructive intensity at work within this man. Jesus had power and authority over it. He was in charge, even over the seemingly uncontrollable forces, and He provided comfort. Jesus brought an internal change to this man that affected who he was externally.

People may be aware of our struggles even if they don't fully understand them. They may even avoid coming near us sometimes. But they may also see God's will working mightily in us when we do the right thing and speak wisely. Then they will be able to see where the real power comes from.

We may not escape every storm, but with Jesus, we can sail through them. We have the mind of Christ written for us in the Bible (1 Corinthians 2:16), and as we apply His will and His words to our hearts and minds, we can say, "It is no longer I who live, but Christ lives in me" (Galatians 2:20 NKJV).

My own mental illness journey has so many emotions, memories, and overwhelming thoughts tied to it that I can't even put it into words.

And that is okay.

"For we do not know what we should pray for as we ought, but the Spirit makes intercession for us with groanings that can't be uttered" (Romans 8:26). God knows me better than I know myself, and when I pray to Him, He helps me in my weakness. When I learn from Him, He helps me see clearly, and His light shines brighter and brighter as the Son rises within me (2 Peter 1:19).

I don't know what tomorrow holds, but I know who holds tomorrow. And He tells me that He will take my hand and comfort me with these words: "Fear not, I will help you" (Isaiah 41:13 NKJV).

The Bible gives us an awareness of mental illness, and, Lord willing, as we continue further along, we will dig deeper to uncover more helpful insights and practices.

Chapter 3

Thoughts

My mind would not shut off. I originally went to see a doctor as an adult because I couldn't fall asleep. The best way I can describe the bombardment of thoughts is this: Imagine driving down a busy city street with your windows rolled down. Traffic is bumper-to-bumper. Cars are honking. Bicyclists are zipping by. An airplane is flying overhead. Construction work is going on. People are yelling. Dogs are barking. Bus air brakes are squealing. A train is rumbling in the distance.

You get the image?

According to the Mayo Clinic, it is very common for people with mental illness to experience racing thoughts, confused thinking, or even a reduced ability to concentrate. It was so loud in my head that I couldn't think straight. When I tried to read, the page's white background came to the forefront instead of the words. That was a very difficult season in my life.

Do you have any similar experiences? Have racing thoughts and trouble concentrating ever surfaced within your mind? How do you deal with those moments?

Thoughts may be like clouds. They can float in and out without a sound, sometimes without us even noticing. Some are thin and wispy, almost invisible. Some are dark, ominous, and full of thunder and lightning. In some of them, we may see shapes. And some are like fog that comes down and engulfs us. It is impossible to consciously create and control every thought, but we are called to direct how we respond to them. Thoughts themselves may not be inherently sinful, but what we dwell on and how we use those thoughts can be (Ephesians 4:26).

How are we to handle our thoughts? Is there anything we can do? Let us look and see what insight God's Word can give us.

"We are destroying arguments and all arrogance raised against the knowledge of God, and we are taking every thought captive to the obedience of Christ" (2 Corinthians 10:5).

We are responsible for conforming our thoughts to submission in Christ. The verse says that we do this by bringing them into captivity. We have to catch them and hold them prisoner. The word *devil* literally means "accuser," so be on guard and capture the thoughts that accuse God or question the validity of His Word and love. If thoughts like that are present, realize that they are not from a good place. Some thoughts we will be able to let pass and float on by, but others will need to be confronted. This will take effort, patience, and awareness on our part. It will be trying at times (James 1:2–4) because many of the thoughts we take for granted may feel as if they are who we really are.

But you are not your mind or your thoughts. That is why we have metacognition, the ability to think about thinking. Thoughts are only one part of us. Some may have been part of our logic and inner life for so long that we have come to believe them. They may run in the background, or we may try to ignore them and block them out of our minds.

I remember when it dawned on me that I could actually change mentally and do things differently. It was both exciting and intimidating.

This won't be easy.

And that is okay.

Just because something isn't easy does not mean it is too hard.

The spirit God supplies gives us the power of a sound mind (2 Timothy 1:7). We saw this exemplified in the demon-possessed man in the previous chapter. According to Strong's Concordance, *Sound Mind* (4995) means self-control or self-discipline. Notice the word *self.* No one can force you to be controlled or disciplined. That is a choice and a responsibility you have to accept. When you choose discipline over your racing thoughts and impulses, and then act according to God's will and might, you are using sound judgment.

If we allow God's words to enter our minds, they will help us reason wisely (Isaiah 1:18). This is especially difficult to grasp when someone has a mood disorder. We have to learn to be swift to hear, slow to speak, and slow to fly off the handle (James 1:19).

It is so much easier to reverse that order.

And that is exactly why we need to capture those thoughts and subject them to God's will and words. Between a stimulus and a response, there is a small space. That space is where we choose our course of words or actions. When we pause, that space grows. And when we place God's words and will above our own, we become more aware, and our thoughts slowly begin to reflect His.

We develop a sound mind by acting out of His words and will, even in the middle of our own loud and chaotic thoughts.

"The god of this world has blinded the minds of the unbelieving so that they will not see the light of the gospel of the glory of Christ, who is the image of God" (2 Corinthians 4:4).

Realize that mental illness is a result of this fallen world and may be used by Satan to blind people to God's truths. When we are immersed in a fog and life seems dreary and dark all the time, it may feel impossible to see the light. Sometimes, hope and a sense of stability can seem unattainable.

When the mind is blind, the eyes will not see.

This is all the more reason to dig into God's words and use them. Start becoming aware of your thoughts. Capture them. Take them prisoner. Hold them up to what God says is real and possible. "Because the mind set on the flesh is hostile toward God; for it does not subject itself to the law of God, for it is not even able to do so" (Romans 8:7).

When we lose sight of God and His purpose for our lives, we turn inward to our own worldly thoughts and plans. That is exactly where Satan wants us to go. He wants us to become enemies of God in our minds. When we focus only on worldly things, our hearts become full of them, and then our mouths speak from that overflow (Luke 6:45).

This is why the Bible encourages us to guard our hearts (Proverbs 4:23), exercise our minds, direct our thoughts, and think on things above (Colossians 3:2).

If we don't arrest our errant thoughts, they can actually imprison us. We may become more concerned with things we can't control while becoming less concerned with what we can control. We may try to micromanage every outcome, scenario, and situation in an attempt to lessen our stress. But in reality, when we do that, we create more pressure and mental fatigue. Realize that when something doesn't go as we planned or hoped, that doesn't mean it is bad or even wrong. God sees our path and our needs. He sends help and guides our steps.

The only true way to have peace is to keep our thoughts directed and our minds trained to focus on God's words, wisdom, insight, and perspective so that we can see above our own limited perceptions (Isaiah 26:3).

When we ruminate on the past or worry about the future, we lose focus on today. To be present is a gift because everything else is only thinking. God allows us to make plans (Luke 13:33), but not at the expense of today. He tells us not to worry about tomorrow because tomorrow will bring its own worries. We can't see the future, but God can, and He tells us today's trouble is enough for now (Matthew 6:34).

So how can we apply this to our lives and minds? Mental illness is not a problem you can simply read about and solve in one sitting, like a math equation. In fact, the verses we have been looking at don't specifically address mental illness. They are instilling proper mindsets and thought processes for rightly dealing with God's word and truth.

So how can we make sense of any of this?

Let us allow God to explain it further.

"Do not be conformed to this world, but be transformed by the renewing of your mind, so that you may prove what the will of God is, that which is good and acceptable and perfect" (Romans 12:2).

Don't be conformed to what? This world.

Satan is the god of this world (2 Corinthians 4:4). The word *satan* literally means "adversary" or "obstruction." So when we don't renew our minds with God's words and apply His will, we allow Satan to run the show and obstruct God's guidance in our lives.

At creation, we saw that God said everything was "very good." And how did God create? He **spoke** it into existence (Psalm 33:9). Words and language shape our minds and perceptions. Words like "hope," "joy," and "peace" expand our mental models of what is possible.

We wouldn't have known God's love unless He had shown it to us through His Word (Ephesians 5:2), and sin appears for what it truly is through the awareness presented in the Bible (Romans 7:7).

What words do you tell yourself? What language consumes your thoughts? Are you aware of them?

If our minds are to be renewed, we must let Jesus, the Word of God (John 1:1), speak into them and allow ourselves to be recreated in His image.

Again, I am not saying that God will instantly heal you of your mental struggles. But know this: good sailors are the ones who go out and battle rough seas. God calls us to follow Him in the midst of our mental storms, for He is the only One who can lead us safely through to the other side (Mark 4:35, 41). Satan only wants us to despair and become shipwrecked on those waters.

The idea of renewal in Romans 12 can be compared to renovating an old home. Imagine going in, bit by bit, removing the old, broken fixtures and replacing them with new ones. Imagine repairing dented walls, scraping and fixing chipped paint, and sanding worn hardwood floors.

The same process is needed in our spiritual house (1 Corinthians 3:16). We replace bad habits, old thought patterns, obsolete attitudes, and harmful actions with God's good and acceptable ways. Hand in hand, we walk with God, allowing Him to complete His work within us (Philippians 1:6).

Each one of us is a unique estate being rebuilt by the Master Craftsman (Hebrews 13:20–21). Allow Him to guide your thoughts, exercise your intellect, and mold you into the image of Christ, even in the midst of your storms.

"Remove the old self and be renewed in the spirit of your mind" (Ephesians 4:22). This will take effort, and we must "prepare our minds for action" (1 Peter 1:13). This isn't about a fresh coat of paint. It is about total restoration to God and transformation through Him, from the inside out.

Catch your thoughts, hold them captive, and submit them to Jesus, **the Word**. *"And the peace of God, which surpasses all comprehension, will guard your hearts and minds in Christ Jesus"* (Philippians 4:7).

Jesus said that "the spirit is willing, but the flesh is weak," so failure is part of the path as long as we are on this earth (Mark 14:38). God has accounted for that in the process, and He helps us along the journey.

We are to avoid doing wrong (Romans 6:1–2), but when we mess up, truly repent (2 Corinthians 7:10) and seek forgiveness, He is faithful to His Word and forgives us (1 John 1:9). We don't truly fail until we refuse to get back up (Hebrews 6:4–6).

I want to encourage you: Keep getting back up. Brave those storms. Use God's words to renew your mind while relying on His might and power to sail through the rough times (2 Timothy 3:5).

Chapter 4

Purpose

I remember seeing a poster on the wall in a preschool classroom at a church's building. It said, *"I know I'm somebody 'cause God don't make no junk."* I read those words, but they didn't automatically transfer to how I felt.

When dealing with a mental disorder, it can be very difficult to feel as though your life has meaning or purpose. You may feel like a social outcast, or "junk", as the poster put it. You might feel isolated from others and completely alone. The belief that nothing will ever improve and that you are destined to fail may overrun your thoughts.

Do you ever equate your success, or your seeming failure, with God's approval? Sometimes we may even become confused and try to use God to fulfill our own purposes rather than aligning ourselves with His. Purpose is not a destination but a daily orientation, and clarity often follows obedience, not the other way around.

In 1 Kings 19, Elijah felt like a failure, an outcast, and completely alone, but that was not God's perspective. Do you ever feel like an outcast? A failure? All alone? God had other plans for Elijah, and He has other plans for you too.

"The LORD said to him, 'Go, return on your way to the wilderness of Damascus; and when you have arrived, you shall anoint Hazael king over Aram. You shall also anoint Jehu the son of Nimshi king over Israel; and you shall anoint Elisha the son of Shaphat of Abel-meholah as prophet in your place'" (1 Kings 19:15–16).

God gave Elijah instructions about where to go and what to do. He also gave him hope by showing him that he wasn't truly alone (verse 18). We have previously discussed the idea of being alone, but what about the topic of purpose?

What is your purpose according to God in light of a mental disorder? Where does He want you to go? What does He call you to do? Have you ever wondered about these questions?

"The mind of a person plans his way, but the LORD directs his steps" (Proverbs 16:9).

What are we to do when our minds don't function well? We may come up with ideas, plans, and strategies. We may even take a guess at the purpose and meaning of our lives, but ultimately, God must be the One who guides us. As long as we acknowledge His will (James 4:13–15) and trust that He is able to strengthen us (Philippians 4:13), we can stay on course. Even when we cannot immediately see the good in a situation, He cares for us and will never leave us or forsake us (Hebrews 13:5).

Do you ever get tunnel vision? Do you ever become so centered on yourself and what you are doing that you lose track of what is going on around you? This can happen in the midst of mental illness, but it can also happen when a person has healthy thought patterns. We can become so caught up in trying to function daily, avoid stress, meet needs, and interact with or avoid others that we lose sight of the bigger picture. *"Life is more than food, and the body is more than clothing"* (Luke 12:23).

Your purpose in life, and even life itself, is far more important and valuable than physical necessities alone. Yet sometimes we may become so overwhelmed that all we can focus on is eating food and finding comfortable pajamas to sleep in.

While God gave Elijah a time of respite, He did not call him to stay there. He called him to travel on. God calls us to do the same. Do not get trapped in the "rest" stage and believe it is the sole purpose of your life or that it is all you can do.

I was stuck in that stage for many, many years. Even when I was on vacation, I would sleep most of the day away in a depressed state. Now, by God's love, grace, and strength, I have been delivered from that shadow land, and I have no intention of ever returning. "Listen, my beloved brothers and sisters; did not God choose the poor in this world to be rich in faith and heirs of the kingdom which He promised to those who love Him?" (James 2:5).

God may allow poverty to be used to help drive a person toward faith. Where else can one go but to the Lord and Creator when in true need (John 6:68)? Are you wondering what all of this has to do with purpose?

It is interesting to note that the word used for "poor" in James 2 refers to someone destitute, but it can also carry the idea of being spiritually poor or humble. It conveys the image of someone dependent on charity. Just as Paul was allowed a thorn in the flesh to keep him spiritually poor, or humble (2 Corinthians 12:7), God may also allow a mental illness in your life so that you may honestly seek Him and rely on His might (2 Corinthians 1:9). When we are dependent on His charity, His love, we can truly find our God-given purpose.

Did you notice why God allows this "poorness" and what the passage in James actually says? So that you can be "rich in faith."

This is one of the paradoxes found in Scripture: when we are poor, we can truly be rich. When a child is learning to walk, they have faith in their parents. They hold tightly to their hands, relying on them for strength and guidance. The child is truly "rich in faith" in their parents because they are “poor” in skill, knowledge, and confidence.

But what eventually happens? They start to walk on their own. Then they start to run. And in their running, they may run ahead of their parents and find that they can run away. When the Israelites received everything they had wanted (Deuteronomy 8:7–14), they ran away from their Father and His loving hands. They became "rich" in worldly possessions, then grew proud and became "poor" in their faith in God.

Does mental illness draw you closer to God in faith? Where are you trying to run away from Him?

I used to get hung up on having a mental illness and see it only as a deficit, but God has shown me how He can use it as an asset. His power has carried me through many mental storms, and my faith has grown exponentially through them.

When we are humble and truly rely on Him for strength and guidance, we allow His might to be shown. We take His hand and let Him lift us up and guide us (Matthew 23:12). But if we allow pride to inflate our egos, we will try to run away, thinking we no longer need Him. Or if we let anxiety crush us and focus only on the wind and waves in the storm, we lose sight of Christ and begin to sink (Matthew 14:30).

The key is not to lose our focus or our dependence on God and His love as we fulfill our purpose.

So what is our purpose?

In Ecclesiastes 12, Solomon concluded that our purpose in life is to revere God and keep His commands. In the New Testament, Jesus spoke of the two greatest commandments: "You shall love the LORD your God with all of your heart, and with all your soul, and with all your mind. This is the great and foremost commandment.

The second is like it, You shall love your neighbor as yourself' (Matthew 22:37–39).

He doesn't give us a list of chores to complete, but a posture toward Him to pursue: love. And it is from that love that our Christian lives should flow (1 John 2:5).

Did you notice what Jesus said is involved in loving God? Our heart, our soul, and our mind. When we renew our minds and are transformed, our hearts are filled abundantly with God's love. That love then floods into our words, our actions, and the very essence of who we are becoming: people God has called out of darkness (1 Peter 2:9).

Our purpose moves from internal to external: heart, soul, and mind, then God and neighbor. He draws us out of ourselves (Proverbs 20:5) and unites us with a higher objective (Mark 10:45). When we find our purpose, we can move from a sitting and lying stage to a standing one, much like Elijah, who moved forward by God's direction and calling.

God calls us to move forward too. He calls us to look beyond food and rest and to realize the greater design for our lives. He supplies everything we need (Philippians 4:19), and His provision far exceeds mere physical sustenance (Matthew 6:33). Through those incredible blessings, we may in turn bless others (Proverbs 11:25–26).

We love Him because He first loved us (1 John 4:19). Our purpose comes from whom we love before it becomes what we do.

We may ask, "What is my purpose in life?" and Jesus tells us to love God fully.

So our true purpose is not simply discovered; it is something we respond to. It is not a point on a map. It is a process. Love God and love your neighbor. Jesus showed us what that love looks like. It is not an emotional, "when I feel like it" kind of love, but a self-sacrificing, giving love that serves even when we don't feel like it.

Our purpose is found in Jesus. When we follow His will and His example, we begin writing new pages in our lives. We grow and stretch beyond our current limitations, gaining confidence in Him and His might. We can then step outside of our own self-focus and become free to serve God and our neighbors in love.

We start learning to love God in action by following Jesus' example. God calls us to love Him with all we have, but if we treat that as a task and only seek to obey, we miss the larger picture. God wants us to know Him. In fact, Jesus came and gave us understanding so that we can know Him (1 John 5:20).

Yes, our love for Him should produce obedience (1 John 5:3), but if we replace God with goals, then our purpose becomes achievement, and our identity becomes performance-based. The purpose God gives us is not only about what we are doing. It is also about who we are becoming.

Our identity is found in Christ (Galatians 2:20), and our value is revealed by God's love for us, shown through the price Jesus paid for our sins (Romans 5:8; Colossians 3:13–14). He loved us when we were at our worst, and He continues to love us as we grow. As we learn to love Him, our hearts and minds are transformed to become more like Christ's, and we can take action with integrity and confidence in His might.

In 1985, my family moved to a new town. I made new friends, and one of them had a swimming pool. His mom said we could swim unsupervised if I could swim the length of the pool and back.

I was so excited.

There was only one small problem: I didn't know how to swim.

So I thought really hard about swimming. I went over it in my mind again and again, practicing and rehearsing the movements as best as I could imagine them. Finally, the day came to try out my abilities. I got into the water, and guess what?

I could not swim.

We can read an entire library about swimming, but until we get into the water, we have not truly moved forward.

This is another deception of Satan: association with something is not the same as transformation (James 1:22). In our minds, we may get excited about the wisdom God offers us, but if we don't pursue it in our lives, we deceive ourselves (Ecclesiastes 11:4). We can read how He gives us purpose and shows us how to love and live, but that must move from mere head knowledge to lived, working wisdom (Proverbs 1:2–3).

Imagine trying to bake a cake, but all you do is read the instructions on the box and take no action. How long would it take before it was ready to eat?

Never. It would never get done.

God calls us to move beyond intention into completion (2 Corinthians 9:2). If we are to love like Christ, it must go beyond religious practices (Matthew 7:21) and being around religious knowledge (Matthew 23:3). God seeks humble and repentant hearts (Psalm 51:7). He calls us to do what is right, show compassion to others, and walk humbly before Him. This means we must be deliberate with our thoughts and actions (Micah 6:8).

We are going to have to love Him with all we've got. Love is a verb, and when we pursue Him through love, we come to know God the Father and Jesus the Christ (John 17:3), are led by the Spirit (Romans 8:14), and grow in the knowledge of Christ (2 Peter 3:18). Through love, we can be known by Him (1 Corinthians 8:3).

So ask yourself: Am I seeking to know God, or am I only looking for instructions from Him?

We can't pursue a new direction while ignoring the current truth. We do not find our purpose by looking inward. We find it by looking upward. Don't confuse busyness with purpose. Ignoring inner transformation while pursuing only outer impact is not God's will. That is exactly what the religious leaders of Jesus' time did.

If we are not busy writing the pages of our own lives, we may stick our noses into other people's stories and try to dictate them, thinking we are truly moving forward.

Where is God showing you that you need to grow closer to Him? Where might you be seeking to follow, but your heart is not fully engaged? What is your current attitude about all of this?

We are called to trust in the Lord with all our hearts and have faith that He will make our paths straight (Proverbs 3:5–6). He doesn't want us to sit around waiting to figure everything out, nor does He want us to micromanage and control every step. He asks us to believe Him, submit, and walk forward.

True purpose is not something we build. It is something we live as we walk with God. We don't find it apart from surrender to His will; we discover it through humble obedience.

God may not tell you which career to pursue or whom to marry, but He gives us guidelines and principles to help us make those choices. He even tells us that our words should convey His love (Ephesians 4:15), and if we serve, we should do so with the strength He supplies (1 Peter 4:11).

You were created on purpose for a purpose. "Therefore, whether you eat or drink, or whatever you do, do all things for the glory of God" (1 Corinthians 10:31).

Chapter 5

Anxiety & Depression

I suffer from Generalized Anxiety Disorder. Even when everything is going well, and life seems normal, I may feel as though my world is in complete chaos and that, at any moment, something terrible is going to happen.

The Bible has many verses on anxiety. These range from doubts and cares (Psalm 94:19) to marriage concerns (1 Corinthians 7:33) to being troubled by sin (Psalm 38:18). While those passages may not deal directly with "mental illness," we can still draw helpful insight from them. "Anxiety in the heart of man causes depression, but a good word makes it glad" (Proverbs 12:25 NKJV).

Anxiety is characterized by excessive worry or fear focused on future danger, whether real or imagined. It can weigh down our feelings, our intellect, and even our will. This can lead to feeling sluggish, worn out, and unmotivated. The text here says that anxiety leads to depression. That is why it is important to deal with anxiety as it comes and not simply wait for it to "get better." God tells us that a good word makes the heart glad, so combating our thoughts with His Word and with proper information can lift us.

"We walk by faith and not by sight in this world" (2 Corinthians 5:7).

Trouble arises when we are driven by anxiety and want to "see" everything first so we can mentally ensure that life is predictable, that there are no surprises, and that everything will be okay. We stop asking, "what is true?" and start asking, "what is safe?"

Here lies an extremely difficult truth to grasp, especially when dealing with mental illness: walking forward in faith means we won't see or know everything first. This is another lie Satan fills our minds with. It is IMPOSSIBLE, as finite human beings, to see and know everything. Only God can do that. When we try to take on that task, we are destined to fail.

Anxiety often highlights where we place our trust. It can reveal what we fear losing and what we believe will protect us. The need for certainty and control can indicate reliance on self, others, or circumstances rather than surrender to God and His guidance. *"Trust in the LORD and lean not on your own understanding"* (Proverbs 3:5).

This is the true essence of faith. In fact, Hebrews says that faith is the evidence of things "not seen" (Hebrews 11:1). If you are only operating on what you currently see, that is not faith. That is leaning on your own intellect. Allow Him to enlighten the eyes of your understanding (Ephesians 1:18).

Walking by faith can give us hope, a hope rooted in knowing that God has better things planned for us than we can even imagine (Ephesians 3:20). I am truly thankful for this because my mind can come up with some terrible scenarios and outcomes. Even my best thoughts pale in comparison to God's grand design and orchestration.

If we could see how everything would turn out, we wouldn't truly be able to have hope. Hope that is seen is not really hope at all (Romans 8:24). So it is a blessing in disguise not to have to trust our own minds and understanding alone, but to rely on God's Word and promises.

I am not saying we should have blind faith. I am saying we should have an educated faith grounded in reality. My mind would always see "danger," "threats," and "trouble" even when none were present. If I were supported only by my own knowledge, I would be a miserable person, and indeed, I was. It may be difficult to filter that kind of reasoning and thinking through God's Word, but that is still the task before us.

It takes hard work, prayer, study, patience, awareness, and discipline to apply this and see His truth. This is a messy process, but with God's might and grace, you can become what He calls you to be. You won't be who everyone else is (2 Corinthians 10:12), and that is okay. God has designed each of us as unique beings, with different abilities, skills, talents, and settings, to effectively carry out His plans (1 Corinthians 12:12ff). His strategy is designed for good, not harm, and it gives us a future and a hope (Jeremiah 29:11).

It is important to understand that what we are discussing may involve more than anxiety caused by a lack of faith. Mental illness can cause anxiety even when we are walking by faith. God is faithful to His promises, and mental illness does not hinder His might (1 Corinthians 1:9). My lack of knowledge or foresight does not mean that God's knowledge is limited.

When I go out to run a few miles, I don't "feel" like doing it. And when I first start running, my body doesn't "want" to. But by God's grace, I have learned discipline, and I have learned that my body will follow my mind. Many times, we may want to wait until we "feel" like doing something before we take action, but God calls us to walk forward in faith, whether we feel like it or not.

In reality, following God and doing the right things should eventually bring about the right feelings. Don't let the feelings of your body override what the Spirit says to do. Jesus, the head of the church, leads the body, not the other way around (Colossians 1:18). The same should be true in our spiritual lives and in our mental warfare. Let the mind of Christ, found in God's Word, lead your body and the actions you pursue. When we rely solely on our own flawed feelings and understanding, we run ahead of God and get lost.

On a run, I may not initially feel like doing it or want to do it. But after I am finished, I am deeply satisfied. I see the benefit of those actions, and I become more competent and confident, knowing that it is possible. All of those "one foot in front of the other" actions turn into miles of learned experience.

I don't think the feeling of "not wanting to" will ever fully go away.

And that is okay.

Even Paul said that he didn't understand some of the things he did and that his body was at war with his mind (Romans 7:15, 23). But he had joy in his inner man because of God's Word, and he knew that true deliverance was found only in Christ (verses 22, 25).

Where are you waiting to "feel like it" before moving? Where do you need to put one foot in front of the other spiritually? Do you let your body control what your mind believes is possible?

You will never be good enough to deserve a home in heaven. You are never going to be perfect on this earth in every thought, word, and action. There was only one perfect Being, and He defeated death so that in Him we can be "more than conquerors" (Romans 8:37).

To conquer something means you are going to have to fight. You are going to have to go to war with your own mind. You are going to have to defeat it with "the sword of the Spirit, which is the Word of God" (Ephesians 6:17). We can overcome through God's might, but we must work together with Him in this conquest (Deuteronomy 31:8). This doesn't mean your mental illness will automatically be removed. That may never happen. But it does mean that in the middle of the fray, you can be more than victorious in God's might.

I am reminded of Samson in the Old Testament, when the Philistines could not figure out where his great strength came from

(Judges 16:5). Have you ever read or heard the stories and pictured Samson as a huge, muscle-bound man? If he had appeared that way, they probably would not have wondered why he was so strong.

This is a helpful example when considering mental illness. You may not feel or even appear mentally "strong." You may even perceive yourself as "weak."

That is okay.

This is another paradox of the Bible. When we are weak, then we can be strong, because God's grace and might can be perfected in us (2 Corinthians 12:9). In the midst of all the chaos and struggle, Samson realized where his true might and ultimate power came from: "Lord GOD, please remember me and please strengthen me" (Judges 16:28).

Samson didn't get his strength from his own body. The Spirit of the Lord gave it to him (Judges 13:25). Don't look down on yourself or let anxiety arise from a perceived lack in your own abilities. This is a perfect opportunity for God's might and strength to fill you. If we are only full of ourselves, there is no room for God to work within us. That is why we need to be spiritually poor and humble. This allows God to raise us up in His might and in His perfect timing (1 Peter 5:6).

Jesus said that "the poor in spirit" are blessed because they are part of the kingdom of God (Matthew 5:3). True joy and peace are given by God through knowing that we are part of His family and that He watches over us and cares for us. We can thank Him for being there for us, even when we weren't there for ourselves.

So ask yourself: *What is it that steals my joy?*

If you're like me, you might attribute it to what is going on around you or even to the people nearby. But God says something different. He tells us that we can have joy even in the middle of difficult and trying times (James 1:2), and that true joy is found in Him (Nehemiah 8:10), not in situations (Habakkuk 3:17–18).

The peace God gives goes beyond physical limitations, and it rules in our hearts through love as we let His Word control the narrative (Colossians 3:14–15). So why do we often lack joy and peace? Because we let doubt and anxious thoughts drive the bus and run right over our faith.

When Jesus was on trial, "false witnesses" came forward to speak against Him (Matthew 26:59ff), and the same can be true within us when His Word is on trial in our hearts and minds. Jesus warns us not to bear false witness (Matthew 19:18). This goes beyond simply lying about someone or a situation in court. Jesus said not to bear false witness because we do lie, even to ourselves.

If you believe, *"I can figure it out"* or *"I don't need help*," are you relying on your own strength and understanding, or are you allowing God room to work within you? We have a very limited view, especially when dealing with mental illness. We need God's perspective to see clearly (Isaiah 55:8–9). If we believe we can guide our own steps (Jeremiah 10:23), then we are fooling ourselves (James 1:16) and running headlong into error (Jude 8–11).

Joy and peace are fruit of the Spirit (Galatians 5:22), and they can't be fully attained through worldly pursuits.

Ask yourself: Am I claiming to let God lead me while anxiously trying to micromanage and control everyone, every scenario, and every outcome?

God cannot lie (Hebrews 6:18) because His Word is truth (John 14:6). So if we are lying to ourselves, that lie comes from Satan, the father of lies (John 8:44). When we try to deal with anxiety apart from God and believe that things will not work out, that nobody understands (Hebrews 4:15), or that nothing can ever change, we are doubting His Word and His care. We are trusting in circumstances, limited views, and lies (Romans 8:15–16).

In doing so, we destroy our opportunity to have joy and peace by choosing anxiety instead of walking in faith in God's might and promises (Philippians 4:6–7). That is exactly how our hearts become crushed (Proverbs 12:25).

The Bible tells us to cast all our anxiety and cares on God because He cares for us (1 Peter 5:7). Mental illness can cause anxiety even when there is no clear cause for anxiety, but He still calls us to move forward even when we do not "feel" like it. His good Word can lift us back up. And when we allow Him to guide us and follow Him in faith, we will have all that we need, even if we cannot immediately see it (Psalm 23:1).

Anxiety Grows

Anxiety can lead to depression, which is marked by persistent sadness, low energy, and a loss of interest in life. Depression can also come in different forms. We have seen situational depression in Elijah, where he struggled to deal with the dramatic changes unfolding in his life. There is also clinical depression, which is a more severe form. This can be caused by drugs or alcohol, genetics, biological factors, environmental factors, or psychological factors.

It is important to note that if situational depression is ignored or not dealt with effectively, it can sometimes progress into clinical depression. Clinical depression can involve imbalances in neurotransmitters that impair nerve communication and may even contribute to reduced neuroplasticity and neurogenesis in the hippocampus.

Did you know that some mental illnesses may be present along with other conditions? This is called comorbidity. I have been diagnosed with treatment-resistant major depression and Generalized Anxiety Disorder. Anxiety and depression can coexist, and I also suffer from Seasonal Affective Disorder and P.T.S.D. This can make things more difficult, not only in medical treatment but also in thinking and processing.

My wife would often say, "*I wonder which Dan we are going to have today.*" My mental functions and moods were up and down like a roller coaster at times. We may have a mental illness or know someone who does, but how much training have we had in dealing with it? Just because we may be familiar with the symptoms does not mean we know the correct path to take in addressing the cause.

I recall one job where I was thrown into a situation with no training. When something went wrong, I froze. I had no idea what to do. My boss pulled me into his office to discuss it. As he was talking, he suddenly said, "*You are doing it right now!*"

One habit I learned as a child was dissociation. Depression, dissociation, O.C.D., avoidant behaviors, and even self-harm may be responses we learned or developed as survival strategies to manage overwhelming stress, pain, or trauma. Some forms of mental illness can function as unhealthy coping mechanisms. Now, I am in no way belittling or downplaying the severity and agony that mental illness can bring. I am simply suggesting that we don't have to receive it as a sentence we must blindly carry out for the rest of our lives.

I am encouraged by Elisha's words in 2 Kings 6. The Syrian army came out to fight against Israel with a great force, with horses and chariots, and surrounded them by night. Elisha's servant saw them and panicked. "What shall we do?" And Elisha answered, "Don't be afraid, for those who are with us are more than those who are with them" (2 Kings 6:15–16 ESV).

He then prayed that God would open his servant's eyes to see the truth. "And he saw, and behold, the mountain was full of horses and chariots of fire all around Elisha" (verse 17 ESV).

When we are with God and His might, greater forces are working with us, for us, and through us than there are against us. God's might is not limited by mental illness, no matter how many struggles may seem to surround you. I pray that God will open your eyes to see the allies and strength working all around you by His guidance.

"My soul is in despair within me; Therefore, I remember you" (Psalm 42:6).

It is not that we will never have struggles or mental unrest, but that we should capture those thoughts, give them to God, and dwell on His might and promises. Depression, whether situational, as in an adjustment disorder, or clinical, as in a mood disorder, needs to be run through God's truth. Let Him divide our thoughts and intentions and straighten them out (Hebrews 4:12).

The Lord is a shelter for those who are crushed and a stronghold in times of trouble (Psalm 9:9). This isn't a mystical freeing from mental illness. Clinical depression is serious and will probably require medical help. This is also not a one-and-done scenario. It is an ongoing posture in life and a process we must hold to. It is understanding where true power and aid come from and relying on Him to supply it.

God calls us out of darkness into His wonderful light (1 Peter 2:9). Sometimes darkness can feel like a gray fog of ***depression*** that settles over us and impairs our spiritual vision. It can be a ***lie*** we believe in place of God's reality. It can be a ***false witness*** that tells us not to trust or believe anything we don't feel or see, but to rely only on our own understanding. It can be a ***doubt*** that wonders whether

God sees us or even cares. After all, if He really did, w*hy did He allow us to have mental illness*?

He does not want us to be ignorant (Hebrews 5:2), and He invites us to reason with Him (Isaiah 1:18) using logic and truth (John 17:17). The problem arises when we ignore His light and choose to hide within our own cave of darkness. When we choose to sit and lie down instead of standing and moving forward toward His call, we deny the true might and power He supplies.

Coming out of the darkness and into the light will expose some things to us. We must be willing not only to see them, but also to deal with them honestly.

Anxiety left unattended can lead to depression, and depression left alone can become more severe. Plant seeds of light and truth using God's Word. Capture your thoughts and become aware of them. Don't water and nurture the unhealthy ones (Philippians 4:8). I encourage you to take up the sword of the Spirit and wield it effectively, accurately handling His truth (2 Timothy 2:15).

Take responsibility for your anxiety and give it to God. Study. Pray. Talk with brothers and sisters in Christ. Seek help from mental health professionals when needed. Don't simply sit back and wait for it to "get better."

If you are struggling with situational or clinical depression, you can cast those cares upon Him too and walk forward in faith. Again, seek medical help when needed. Don't wait until you "feel" like it. If nothing changes, then nothing changes. Take action with confidence placed in Him.

He invites us to change our posture, and in doing so, He will transform us from the inside out, even if we still have a mental illness. I pray that God enlightens your eyes to see the good all around you.

Chapter 6

Hope

How often do you think about heaven? Do you long to be there one day? Does it put joy in your heart to dwell on God's promises concerning it?

I have had great difficulty believing that I am going there. My anxiety disorder makes me feel as though I am doomed and will not spend eternity with my heavenly Father. This is especially troubling because, as a Christian, I am supposed to be able to have hope, so much so that I am willing to give an account for it and even defend it (1 Peter 3:15).

What exactly is hope? When you hear that word, what comes to mind? What do you associate hope with? Where does it come from?

Biblical hope is not wishful thinking. It is not blind optimism or a vague feeling that the universe will provide what is needed. True, lasting hope is rooted in God's Word, not human emotion. We do not manufacture hope; we receive it through His revelation of truth. Hope is a confident expectation anchored in God's character (Hebrews 6:18–19), His promises (Titus 1:2), and the resurrection of Jesus (1 Peter 1:3).

"Now may the God of all hope fill you with joy and peace in believing, so that you will abound in hope by the power of the Holy Spirit" (Romans 15:13).

Notice the process Paul describes here. Where does hope come from? God. And how does the inspired apostle say it is added to us? By the power of the Holy Spirit.

This is not a mysterious, overwhelming event. It is part of the continuous process that the Christian life should possess. I do not deny that the Spirit is alive and active, but I do know that the Bible says we have a part in this process. This happens through believing God and His Word.

The apostle John said he was writing so that his audience might know they have eternal life (1 John 5:13). And yet, my mental illness constantly steals my feeling of hope and disrupts my thinking when I consider heaven.

This is exactly where faith comes into play. I may not "feel" like I have everlasting life waiting for me, but the Lord God Almighty tells me that I do. So I have a choice: either move forward toward His calling or sit and lie down with my "feelings."

Feelings are not facts.

Faith comes from hearing God's Word (Romans 10:17), and it is through faith that we overcome this world (1 John 5:4). His Word is not lacking in power to save (Romans 1:16), and it will accomplish its purpose (Isaiah 55:11). This does not mean, however, that every person who hears God's message will receive it and have hope (Matthew 13:15).

"For we also received the good news just as they did; but the message they heard was of no value to them, since they did not share the faith of those who comprehended it" (Hebrews 4:2 BSB).

We are beings of free will and choice. Depending on the condition of the soil of our hearts (Matthew 13:18–23), we either let His words pierce through (Acts 2:37), or we become hardened and deflect them (Acts 7:54). We can choose to ignore His message of hope (Romans 1:21), suppress the truth (Romans 1:18), be blinded (2 Corinthians 4:4; Mark 4:12), or even believe it but refuse to openly adhere to it (John 12:42).

Or we can choose to sit at His feet in the middle of busy and worrisome events and listen to Him (Luke 10:41–42).

So which will you choose? Which do you currently choose? This determines whether you can have real hope, and that choice is a daily decision (Luke 9:23).

Have you ever wondered how someone loses hope? Have you ever experienced that, or have you seen someone who has? A person can go from vibrant and alive to crushed and despondent. It is not necessarily the events that happen, but what we tell ourselves about those events. It is what we tell ourselves about God and His love for us, and what we believe are the possible outcomes, as though we could see all available options.

Let us look at a biblical event that clearly shows this process.

Paul was sent off to Rome (Acts 25:10ff), and he boarded an Alexandrian ship carrying grain (Acts 27:6). The wind was contrary, and they sailed slowly and with ***difficulty*** for many days. When the wind no longer allowed them to travel their current course, they took a ***detour*** (Acts 27:7–8).

Do you ever make plans or have ambitions and then set out to achieve them? Have you ever come up against obstacles that changed your course? What did you think? How did you respond? What do you tell yourself when things do not go as you think they should? And where is hope in all of this?

After a considerable amount of time, Paul's voyage became ***dangerous*** because it was late in the season and the seas were rough (Acts 27:9). Paul tried to warn them: "Men, I perceive that the voyage will certainly be with damage and great loss" (verse 10). He told them they would not only lose the cargo and the ship, but also their lives. But ***other voices***, false witnesses in a sense, chimed in and decided to go against sound wisdom.

When we face a decision, do we listen to God's voice or to other voices? We should certainly seek counsel (Proverbs 11:14), but how many decisions or paths do we pursue by our "feelings" alone, or by our own wisdom and understanding? We certainly have a say in our lives, but if we ignore God's words, we will suffer shipwreck (1 Timothy 1:19).

"When a moderate south wind came up, thinking they had attained their ***purpose,*** *they weighed anchor and began sailing along Crete"* (Verse 13).

Do you ever pursue a course believing you have found your purpose? Is that direction in line with God's wisdom or contrary to it? We may feel that things are going well and fool ourselves into thinking there really is hope and that the danger is gone.

"But it was not long before a cyclone called the Northeaster swept down across the island" (Verse 14 BSB). "And when the ship was caught in it and could not head into the wind, we ***gave up*** and let ourselves be driven" (Verse 15).

How long does it take for you to give up in life and let yourself be pushed along? What does it take? What is the last straw?

They were able to get the ship under control with ***great difficulty***. They then used ropes to wrap around the ship's hull to try to ***hold it together*** (verses 16–17). "Fearing that they may run aground on the shallows of Syrtis, they let down the sea anchor and let themselves be driven along" (verse 17).

They were now only reacting to the storm, trying to keep everything from falling apart and ***fearing the worst***. The next day, the storm was so violent that they threw out the cargo (verse 18). This voyage had gone forward contrary to an experienced voice of warning. They had set out to make a profit from selling grain in

Rome and to deliver the prisoners, but now their original intentions and purposes had shifted greatly.

On the third day, they threw the ship's tackle into the sea with their own hands (verse 19). The truth had now settled in. They had given up on trying to direct their course entirely. They were accepting the fate of their previous choices and direction. They were now only ***drifting along***.

Do you see the slow path these men had been traveling? Do you see the clear warning they had been given but chose to ignore? What were the results of their lack of discretion? Where was hope?

"Since neither the sun nor stars appeared for many days, and no small storm was assailing us, from then on ***all hope*** of our being saved was ***slowly abandoned***" (verse 20).

They went from fearing the loss of profit and deliveries to facing the possibility that their very lives might be lost. That is a stark contrast from their original starting point. The sun and stars had disappeared. They were not just sources of light; they were how ancient sailors navigated on open waters. They had gone from trying to guide themselves to being unable to do so at all. They ***lost all hope*** that anything good could come from this.

Did you see the progression?

They had worldly hope and set out with purpose to reach a desired destination. Then difficulty came, so they took a detour. The journey brought serious complications and danger, yet they listened to other voices instead of wisdom. Progress seemed to improve for a moment, but before long, they were caught in a huge storm and gave up. They faced great adversity and were only trying to hold things together. Then they began to fear the worst and simply drifted along. Finally, they saw no light, only darkness, and hope was slowly abandoned.

Can you relate to this process? Have you ever lost hope in an endeavor? Where do you find hope? Has it ever seemed as though you couldn't see any light in a situation?

Is it possible to have hope even in the middle of such devastating events?

Absolutely.

"Take heart, men. For I have faith in God that it will be exactly as I have been told" (Acts 27:25 ESV).

Paul, in the middle of this catastrophic storm, encouraged others with the true hope he had been given by God. An angel comforted Paul and told him that none of them would lose their lives (verse 22). If they had listened a few weeks earlier, none of this would have happened (verse 21).

How many times, in the face of our crushed worldly hopes, do we lose sight of God's true hope and lose the light given by His guiding words and wisdom? How many of our storms are brought about because we did not listen to wise counsel and only followed our own feelings or understanding? Or maybe we listened to other voices instead of God's words. Sometimes people make a mess of their lives and then blame God (Proverbs 19:3). But God saves lives, here and in eternity.

This was not the first shipwreck Paul had encountered, both physically (2 Corinthians 11:25) and spiritually (1 Timothy 1:15, 19). He had come out on the other side by God's might and grace, and now he was able to encourage others in the midst of their storm (2 Corinthians 1:4), the very same storm he was currently in.

Sometimes we are allowed to go through tough times and struggles not only to see God's deliverance, but also to help others see light in the darkness.

"In hope against hope he believed" (Romans 4:18).

This is the real tension we are discussing in this chapter. We can have hopes in this world. In fact, God allows us to make plans and pursue them, but we must remember that the outcome is in His hands (James 4:13–16).

In the Old Testament, Abraham realized that Sarah was beyond childbearing years, so by worldly standards, hoping to have a child was impossible (Romans 4:19). But he understood that true, lasting hope is found in keeping our eyes on things above, even when physical hope seems to fall apart (John 8:23).

Abraham focused on God's wisdom and trusted what He said was possible in the face of adversity. Through God's love, we can see beyond earthly profits and recognize spiritual gains (Acts 16:19). If we place our hope only in this life and in this world, then we will be truly miserable (1 Corinthians 15:19).

God offers hope in the middle of our severe storms, even when everything around us looks lost and dark. He does not say life will be easy or free from difficulty. Jesus actually says the opposite (John 16:33). There will be many hard and trying times (Job 14:1).

Paul was allowed by God to be in situations where he was under great pressure and pushed far beyond his ability to endure, so much so that he thought he would not survive (2 Corinthians 1:8).

Still, he had real hope in the middle of what looked like hopelessness. The true hope God offers is not based on everything going the way we think it should. It is based on believing that His Word is true and that His promises and might will help us overcome.

Where we place our hope reveals what we entrust with our meaning, our sense of worth, and our purpose (1 Peter 4:19). Are you seeking to gain "treasure" here, or are you storing it up in heaven (Matthew 6:20)? Are you trying to dig up lasting fulfillment and a sense of completeness on this earth? Those are things found only in Christ (Colossians 2:12–13).

When we know that He sees us, wants the best for us, and guides our steps (Psalm 119:105), then we can have confidence that He will cause all things to work together for good (Romans 8:28). Even if that means we may perish physically, we can still overcome spiritually (Daniel 3:17–18).

We are all pilgrims passing through this world. For us, to live is Christ, and to die is gain (Philippians 1:21). God loves Jesus, and yet He allowed Him to die. Statistically, ten out of ten people die. It is an appointment we all will meet, and we cannot stop it (Hebrews 9:27). But we can hold on to God's hand in humility and come out victorious on the other side.

There were many times in my depression when I had lost hope in this world, but hope in heaven pulled me through. I will repeat it: God's hope saves lives, here and in eternity (Romans 8:24–25).

"Now faith, hope, and love remain" (1 Corinthians 13:13).

As we love God and put faith in Him, we can grow in hope and know that He has everything under control. Hope produces faith and love (Colossians 1:5), and faith produces joy and peace, which lead to hope (Romans 15:13). That may sound confusing, even like circular reasoning, but it is simply truth as God has designed it.

We have an initial hope in God's gift of Christ and a home in heaven. As we believe and follow Him, He gives us joy and peace. That gives us stability, which allows hope to overflow within us as we come to know that He makes all things beautiful in His time (Ecclesiastes 3:11).

We can't try to have hope while ignoring all that God gives, because love, joy, and peace are fruit of the Spirit through faith (Galatians 5:22). We must receive His truth and believe it, allowing it to transform our hearts, minds, and lives. When this happens, our hope will grow even greater.

When the hope God gives defines your future, you can be freed from the burden and frustration of relying on everything in this life turning out exactly how you wish it would. That won't happen.

And that is okay.

In the face of struggles and suffering, holding on to His hope can reorient our hearts and minds. We can have joy and peace out on those open seas by focusing on true, lasting hope.

God is a source of light for those in darkness (Matthew 4:16). He shines, and darkness cannot overcome Him (John 1:5). We may struggle with mental illness and feel immersed in "darkness," but God gives hope even when things look lost and hopeless.

The hope He provides is an anchor that is sure, steadfast, and solid (Hebrews 6:19), because what we may consider impossible is possible with God (Luke 18:27).

I encourage you to take hold of the lasting hope He offers.

Chapter 7

Fear

I was afraid of everything. In public, I couldn't even look at little children because they don't look away like most adults do. They just stare at you, as if they are looking right into your soul.

I was a big, burly man on the outside, weighing 399 pounds, but inside I was broken and crushed. Fear was a hostile enemy that had taken residence within me, and it drove most of my thoughts and actions, or lack thereof.

How much does fear drive your life? Once you start seeing it for what it truly is, you might be surprised.

It was always someone or something else's fault that I wasn't progressing more in life, whether emotionally, relationally, financially, physically, or mentally. Sure, I had a job, a family, and a home, but I was not being proactive. I was mainly just reacting to what I thought was required of me.

Fear kept me small.

Fear of the unknown. Fear of being uncomfortable. Fear of not knowing where I really stood, whether in my convictions, socially, or with God. Fear of being found out as a fraud. Fear that others would see I didn't really know it all or have everything under control. Fear of climbing the mountains God had called me to overcome.

Fear narrows our lives, and when it controls the narrative, we will not take responsibility for ourselves.

There is a Greek proverb that says, *"Self-control makes the man. A man without discipline is a boy full of reactions, rather than a man of good actions."* I looked like a man on the outside, but by my thoughts and actions, I was a child on the inside. I was being driven along in my mental storms and was not truly trying to control my vessel. I was only trying to hold it all together.

Sure, I believed in God and tried not to sin, but I was under the illusion that if I simply sat back and waited, God would take care of everything Himself. I allowed fear to keep me hidden in the dark and sheltered within. All the while, God was calling me to come out into the light and stand upon that mountain.

Let us look at a biblical example of fear taking hold.

In Genesis, God placed man in the garden, and everything was very good. He gave man provision, purpose, direction, relationship through Eve, and communion with Himself. There was perfection on earth, until there wasn't.

We know the story of the temptation, the eating of the forbidden fruit, and the fall. But how well do you know the story of fear that goes along with it?

Adam and Eve were separated from God by their sin, and when they heard Him coming in the garden, they hid. Why? Why would they try to hide from God and His presence? Adam said, "I heard Your voice in the garden, and I was afraid because I was naked; and I hid myself" (Genesis 3:10). Fear had now come to paradise, and it brought with it a desire to hide from God and from view. Adam was no longer seeking to be in the light of God's presence, but fleeing from it.

God asked Adam how he knew he was naked, and Adam again reacted with a fear-based response, "The woman that You gave to be with me, she gave me of the tree, and I ate" (Verse 12).

Did you notice what Adam said? He placed responsibility for his sin on Eve and even on God Himself. Yet the Bible is very clear about where the true guilt lies. Eve was indeed deceived and tricked by the serpent, but Adam was not (1 Timothy 2:14).

"So, when the woman saw that the tree was good for food, and that it was pleasant to the eyes, and a tree desirable to make one wise, she took of its fruit and ate" (Genesis 3:6). Satan was very clever. He twisted God's words, and Eve fell to his scheme (1 John 2:16).

"She also gave to her husband with her, and he ate" (verse 6).

Did you catch it? Eve was tricked, but Adam was right there, and he simply went along with her. Her vision was clouded, but he sinned with his eyes wide open. And when God later confronted him about this, Adam refused to take responsibility and became a blame-shifter.

What are some areas of your life where you place blame? What situations or people do you give free rein to? Where do you take the passenger's seat in your own life?

God calls husbands to love their wives, lead them, and help watch over and protect them so they may be preserved (Ephesians 5:22ff). We are to love as Christ loves His church, even if that means laying our lives down for them (John 15:13).

Many men may say they would die for their wives, but how many would live for them? How many fail to stand up for what is right because they fear their wife's reaction or do not want to make waves? The phrase "a happy wife is a happy life" should never rule out God's will (Acts 5:29).

Adam failed to lead, failed to protect, and failed to keep his wife from dying spiritually. Then he tried to throw her and God under the bus.

Let me ask: Are these the actions of a man or the reactions of a boy?

Fear is a terrible guide for our lives. The more clearly we can see fear working within us, the more opportunity we have to confront it. It has been said that if you don't understand someone, you will misunderstand them. This includes our own fearful selves.

Fear is so prevalent in our world today that you may not even notice its subtle treachery. For example, it is a huge motivator in the sales market. The next time you are in a store, notice how many fear-based messages are presented: "Limited-time offer," "Last chance," "Special edition," or "Rare." These phrases are everywhere.

Even items that appear to be a great deal can drive fear-based responses. "Buy one, get one free" (BOGO) and "Buy three, get the fourth free" are great examples. Retail markets are not profitable because they simply give items away. They persuade you to buy more. You may spend more on a premium item, or even three times your original intention, because you fear missing out (FOMO).

So what exactly is fear?

In the Bible, the Greek word is "*phobos*," the root word that gives us the English word "phobia." According to Strong's Concordance (5401), it conveys the idea of fleeing, running away, or avoiding because of dread, as well as the feeling of having inadequate resources. Fear creates scarcity in our minds, as seen in sales tactics, and can cause us to believe that our wants are actually needs.

"God has not given us the spirit of fear, but of power and of love and a sound mind" (2 Timothy 1:7 NKJV).

This type of fear is seen as a lack of trust in God's might and power, a "lack of resources" by our estimation. Fear kept the ten spies from taking what God said was theirs (Numbers 13:31). Then they told others it was not possible, and because of their lack of faith, the whole nation fell under fear and wandered in the wilderness for decades (Numbers 14:33–34).

God abundantly supplies what is needed (Philippians 4:19), though that is not the same as giving us everything we want. Our lack of faith can hinder what He provides (James 1:5–6). This is not a prosperity gospel, but a real and living faith that relies upon God.

Where does a lack of faith in God show up in your life? What are you wondering, and where are you wandering because of it?

The Bible tells us that fear involves torment (1 John 4:18). When we allow fear to take control of our minds, we tell ourselves that we are going to suffer some kind of punishment if we do or don't do something.

"If I don't _______, then they won't like me." ***Suffering.***
"If that happens, then everything will be ruined." ***Suffering.***
"If I mess up, then I won't know how to _______." ***Suffering.***

Do you see the pattern?

Fear can cause anxiety, panic, and timidity concerning people, circumstances, or the future. We can allow fear to lead us into catastrophic or black-and-white thinking and drive us inward, into the dark.

Very often, what we fear in our minds never even occurs. How many times have you dreaded something and made a situation much worse in your mind, only to find out later that it was not really that bad? When mental illness is present and mood disorders are at work, these effects can be even more pronounced.

I encourage you to move forward. Come out and stand in the light.

"My friends, do not be afraid of those who kill the body, and after that have nothing more that they can do. But I will warn you whom to fear: fear the One who, after He has killed someone, has the power to throw that person into hell" (Luke 12:4–5).

Did you ever touch something hot as a child? You may have been told not to do it, but you did not have a healthy respect for or knowledge of the consequences. So you were fearless, and you did it anyway. And what happened? You made it a point not to do that again, right? You learned the hard way.

God's Word and wisdom show us the consequences ahead of time and point us toward a healthy fear. He does not want anyone to perish and learn too late (2 Peter 3:9).

The Bible tells us to fear God. So how does that make sense? If He does not give us a spirit of fear, why are we told to fear Him? Isn't fear bad? Where does fear come from?

Fear is a choice. We may need to learn to choose healthy fear and unlearn unhealthy fear.

I used to be afraid of dark waters, such as rivers and lakes. My mind would race with thoughts of unseen creatures, logs, deep holes, and more. Hanging out by a body of water was not a typical family outing, and since I had never really learned to swim, I had very little exposure to it.

So later in life, I bought a kayak and set out to overcome my fear. But before I put it into moving water, I decided to try it out at a small park with a pond and a waterway just off the river. I got into the kayak, shoved off, and started paddling. I reached one end, turned around, and right in the middle, my worst fear happened: I tipped over and fell out of the kayak into dark water. I stood up, the water a little over waist-deep, covered in slime and weeds. Once it happened, I realized that I had made it far more terrifying in my mind than it actually was. After that, I was not so afraid of the river, and I was free to venture farther from my comfort zone.

Unhealthy fear involves punishment, but when we fear the Lord and follow Him, we walk in love, knowing that we have a home waiting in heaven. The fear, respect, and awe that we learn and hold for God should help keep us from sinning (Exodus 20:20), and it points to eternal life (Proverbs 19:23). It is a terrifying thing to fall into the hands of the living God (Hebrews 10:31), but as His children, we are not falling into His hands; we are holding on to them and letting Him guide and raise us.

We have hope through His character, His Word, and Jesus' sacrifice, and we can boldly approach His throne, knowing that He hears us and helps us in times of need (Hebrews 4:16). A healthy reverence for the Lord brings confidence and reassurance because the fear of the Lord is the beginning of wisdom (Proverbs 1:7). This is not earthly wisdom. Fearing God will not automatically turn you into an astrophysicist. No, the wisdom God supplies may even seem crazy by worldly standards: "You are insane, Paul! Much learning turns you to insanity!" (Acts 26:24 BLB).

The wisdom of this world is foolishness in comparison to God's wisdom (1 Corinthians 3:19), because human wisdom does not truly reveal Him (1 Corinthians 1:21) and can darken hearts and understanding (Romans 1:21). We know that we are from God, but the world lies under the power of the evil one (1 John 5:19), and he blinds people to the truth (2 Corinthians 4:4).

God's wisdom shines on us, and He lovingly calls us to walk out of the darkness of fear and into His light.

Darkness, according to Strong's Concordance (4653), can refer to moral or spiritual obscurity that blocks the light of God when faith is lacking. We are to have a healthy fear of the Lord, but if we have unhealthy fear, we are actively blocking the light God offers. If we have fear rooted in doubt of God's love or ability, or if we allow the fear of others to keep us from following Him, we are setting ourselves up for failure. *"The fear of man brings a snare, but whoever trusts in the LORD shall be safe"* (Proverbs 29:25 NKJV).

Again, when dealing with mental illness, fear or anxiety may still be present even while walking by faith. The message is still the same: look toward His light. "There is no fear in love, but perfect love drives out fear" (1 John 4:18).

Notice that fear must be driven out. It is within every one of us (2 Corinthians 7:5). It has been suggested that human infants are born with two innate fears: the fear of falling and the fear of loud noises. All other fears are believed to be acquired later through experience and influence, affected by age and amygdala connectivity.

Initially, we may not have certain fears, like the child and the stove, until we get burned. By the time one reaches adulthood, many fears have accumulated. Some are real, and some are imagined. It is not that we will ever be free from all fear, but that as we walk forward in God's love, we don't leave room for fear to control our lives.

There are some healthy, rational fears, such as angry barking dogs or the presence of violence. I would be afraid to walk in front of a speeding locomotive, as I should be. A prudent person sees danger and steps aside (Proverbs 27:12). But there are also unhealthy fears, such as scarcity mindsets and black-and-white or catastrophic thinking.

Fear can range from mild to moderate. It usually involves the presence of danger and should be dealt with in a healthy way as soon as possible.

What fears do you currently hold? How many of them come from your childhood perception? Which ones are still valid today? Where do you need to take action in God's love and drive out unhealthy fear?

An even greater struggle comes when a temporary fear reaction to real or perceived danger becomes extreme, irrational, and persistent. That fear has now become a *phobia*, an anxiety disorder.

Phobias often come from trauma, learned behavior, or conditioned automatic negative reactions to specific objects or situations. They may be extreme and can be triggered simply by thinking about, speaking about, or expecting the object or situation. They can also lead to avoidance behaviors that disrupt daily life. If you suspect you have a phobia, medical intervention or counseling may be needed.

Have you ever heard the phrase, "Hindsight is 20/20"? Do you know why that is?

When we are in the moment, we are full of emotions. We have a lot going on. We are under stress. We have limited knowledge, and we don't see the end clearly, if at all. But after the fact, outside of that moment, emotion, and limited knowledge, we can see more accurately. Then we may have an "Aha!" moment.

God does not live within time (1 Timothy 1:17). God is not ruled by emotion alone, but by power, might, and a sound mind. He is not lacking in knowledge (Psalm 139:4). He declares the end from the beginning, and from ancient times He reveals things that were still to come (Isaiah 46:10). God never says, "*I didn't see that coming*!"

For Him, nothing is about to happen, and nothing has just happened. Everything is before Him. If we hold to Him, His words, and His guidance, we can save ourselves a lot of heartache.

So God tells us not to have unhealthy fear and to drive it out. How can we do that?

Capture those thoughts (2 Corinthians 10:5). Learn to pause after a stimulus and not respond so quickly. Listen to what you are telling yourself (James 1:19). No one is going to take fear away from you. It is your responsibility to own it, though this does not apply to abusive situations. Hold those thoughts up to what God says is possible. Seek godly counsel. Pray and ask God Himself for wisdom (James 1:5). If you are suffering from extreme fears or phobias, seek professional help.

"So, we don't lose heart. Though our outer self is wasting away, our inner self is being renewed day by day" (2 Corinthians 4:16).

Renew your mind with God's light. If you don't know how to do something, research it and learn. Desire without knowledge is not good (Proverbs 19:2). It may be beyond your skills or abilities, so ask for help from others (Joshua 15:16). If you need professional help, seek it out (Luke 5:31). Don't simply sit back and wait for everything to work itself out. Yes, we are to have patience, but not with eyes blinded by ignorance (Hosea 4:6).

Consider what fear does: it creates scarcity, turns wants into needs, drives us inward, and leads to catastrophic or all-or-nothing thinking. Capture those thoughts and hold them up to the light. If our minds and hearts are darkened, we should not go further inside ourselves. We need to get outside and gain a different perspective.

We can't solve a math problem without all the variables, constants, coefficients, and terms. Yet we may try to solve problems in our heads without complete information and then assume the answer is correct. Satan uses many schemes, so why should we lie to ourselves (Proverbs 19:5)? A healthy respect for God leads to wisdom (Psalm 111:10). We may never see all the information, but if we make decisions without wisdom, that is called foolishness.

If you have a scarcity mindset, take an honest assessment of what is truly needed in a situation and consider what demands you are placing upon it. Notice the places where your wants have become needs. Take time to reflect on and consider all the blessings God has allowed into your life.

God tells us to give thanks in all situations and to rejoice always (1 Thessalonians 5:16–18), which means even in difficult times, as they can be blessings in disguise. When we focus on gratitude, it can help shift activity away from the amygdala, the fight-or-flight response, and toward the prefrontal cortex, where logic and reasoning occur. It is generally not possible to feel deep gratitude and intense fear at the same time.

Paul and Silas were beaten, thrown into jail, and put into stocks (Acts 16:24ff), and in the middle of that chaos, they sang to God and prayed to Him. "And the prisoners were listening" (verse 25).

Again, those around Paul, in a dark and hopeless place, were allowed to see God's light through his actions and words. Let your light shine amid your dark storms so that others can see God's strength and love pushing the fear out. Then they can glorify Him (Matthew 5:16). Have you ever considered that when others see a great change and turnaround in your life by God's might, they can glorify Him because of you (Galatians 1:24)?

If you have catastrophic thinking or black-and-white, all-or-nothing thinking, capture those thoughts. Hold those dark thoughts up to God's light. Dwell on what is true. Dwell on what is just. Dwell on what is commendable. Dwell on what is good (Philippians 4:8). Learn to listen to His promises. Think on His character and His love for you. Consider all the difficulties and rough places He has carried you through.

Grab those dark thoughts and light 'em up.

This is not just positive affirmation, though it does have its place. This is shooting holes in the darkness with light and replacing old software with updated, better programming.

These are not quick fixes, one-and-done solutions, or instant cures. This posture and attitude must be developed. This is a process that must be consciously applied over and over until it becomes ingrained and second nature. To conquer in Christ, you are going to have to go to war with your thoughts.

In addition, if you are dealing with severe fears or phobias, you may still need to seek professional help. We can't blame others or circumstances and expect to gain ground.

I have prayed for many years that God would take away my mental illness, and He hasn't done it. BUT I have sought professional help, and through His word, might, and power, I have learned ways to challenge my thoughts, develop new ways of thinking, hold myself accountable, become disciplined, and much more.

I still have mental illness, but it is more manageable now for my family and me. It is a thorn in the flesh that helps keep me humble and on my toes, both physically and spiritually. Sometimes God heals, and sometimes He doesn't. But He always gives us the skills, resources, and opportunities we need. Sometimes our answered prayer means God gives us a tool and then says, *"Get to work."*

We all have fears, some healthy and some unhealthy, some imagined and some real. And we all have opportunities to let God fight alongside us, lifting us when we can't stand and shining light when all we see is darkness. We all have battles that may seem impossible. But in those moments, ask yourself, *"Whose eyes am I seeing through?"*

"Fear not, little flock, for it is your Father's good pleasure to give you the Kingdom" (Luke 12:32 ESV).

When the Lord is with you, He will help you drive out those thoughts of fear, the enemy within (Joshua 14:12). I encourage you to take up your sword, His Word, go to battle, and drive out unhealthy fear in love.

Chapter 8

Anger

"It was an accident." I said that a lot. In my lack of discretion and blind rage, I broke many things, including my family's trust and their sense of safety in my presence.

Anger doesn't just surface because of what happened. It also surfaces because of what we think about what happened. It exposes what we value most, where our expectations are unmet, and even where pride, control, or fear may be rooted.

Ask yourself: What does my Anger consistently point to in my life? What am I protecting when I get angry? Do I bring my Anger to God, or do I justify it within myself?

Anger is a signal, but it should never become our master. Feeling angry is human, but stewarding anger is a spiritual matter because, left unchecked, it can distort truth.

"Do not make friends with an angry person, and don't be a companion of a hot-tempered man, or you will learn his ways and entangle yourself in a snare" (Proverbs 22:24–25 HCSB).

Anger is contagious. It can be a natural physiological response to threats, but how it is expressed is learned through behavioral modeling, reinforcement, and socialization, primarily during childhood. It gradually rewires your reactions, shortens your emotional fuse, and can distort your perception of others. You don't just witness Anger; you begin to adopt its patterns. You may think you are choosing your responses, but over time, reactions can become automatic. Then you are trapped.

How does Anger work? What is actually going on within us?

Before rational thought, or deliberate conscious reasoning, even comes online, your body is already busy interpreting and reacting. This happens through fast, automatic systems tied to survival, including the limbic system and the amygdala.

1. We start with ***Raw Sensory Impressions*** (pre-interpretation). These are not thoughts but just data. Visual flashes, sounds, physical contact, and smell. At this stage, your brain is asking, *"What is this?"*

2. Next comes ***Body Sensations*** (interoception), and your body starts reacting before you consciously "decide" anything. Tightness in the chest, muscle tension, increased heart rate, or

breathing. This is your nervous system scanning for safety or danger.

3. Then, there are ***Emotional Sparks*** (pre-verbal emotions). These are proto-emotions; they arise before you can name them. Unease (sense something is "off"), irritation (before Anger), dread (before fear), warmth (before affection), attraction (before desire). These are generated rapidly via circuits like the amygdala, often before the prefrontal cortex evaluates anything.

4. Next are ***Reflexive Action Urges***; your body begins preparing immediately, and you lean back or pull away. Leaning forward or focusing in. Fight, Flight, or Freeze.

5. Next, we have ***Pattern* Recognition** (subconscious). Your brain rapidly matches what's happening to past experiences. "This feels like that time" (unconsciously stated). Biases activate. Assumptions begin forming silently. This is fast, automatic, efficient, but sometimes inaccurate.

6. Finally, we see ***Emotional Labeling*** (thought engages). Only after ALL of that does rational thought begin: "I'm angry," "That was disrespectful," "I feel anxious." At this point, your prefrontal cortex is trying to interpret what the body has already started.

We don't start with logic first. We start with sensation, emotion, interpretation, and then reasoning. So by the time you think, your body has already detected, felt, reacted, and leaned toward action. All of this happens almost instantly.

If anger is our default response, it can be expressed with little to no thought. That is why we are to guard our hearts and minds (Proverbs 4:23), because the outflow of our emotions, thoughts, and actions is sourced from them (Luke 6:45). If we have good material to use, then our thinking processes and actions can be built upon solid ground and not only on the shifting sands of our "feelings."

Anger is not one-size-fits-all. There can be situational Anger, which is tied to a trigger, or mood-driven Anger, which arises internally. It is important to keep in mind that with some mental illnesses, several systems may be altered. There may be increased threat sensitivity, a hyperactive amygdala, reduced impulse control, reduced prefrontal regulation, and faster emotional escalation.

When Anger is present because of a mood disorder, there may not be a logical explanation or cause that can be pinpointed. The irritation may be present because of poor diet, lack of sleep, not enough physical movement, medications, drugs, alcohol, or even a dysregulated nervous system. Or it may be none of those. You may be irritable and on edge for days, and then it goes away suddenly, like a fever breaking in the night. You may "wake" and feel better emotionally and mentally, but worn out physically.

If it is from a mood disorder, it will not always make sense. That is why it is called a disorder.

Have you ever heard someone say, *"It's not my fault"*, or *"They made me angry"*? Anger is often a protective response that masks vulnerability. Fear says: "I might be hurt," but Anger says: "I will not be hurt." Anger arises quickly because it feels stronger than fear. Fear can be a motivator for Anger, and just like in the garden, it can cause a person to hide and refuse to take responsibility for their actions.

God says it is possible to be angry and not sin, but to do that, we must own it (Ephesians 4:26). He says we can control it, and that should offer us hope. **What we do with our Anger is a choice**. We are going to have to do difficult things and put in the effort to overcome our poor learned responses of Anger, much like learning healthy eating habits.

Is there hope for someone with a mental illness to overcome this reaction? God says there is.

This is a battle, not a stroll through the park.

And that is okay.

God is a mighty warrior (Revelation 19:11–16) who fights for us (Exodus 14:14), alongside us (Deuteronomy 20:1–4), and within us as we are filled with Christ (Galatians 2:20). It is in Him and His Spirit that we are victorious, especially in the storms of mental illness (Zechariah 4:6).

So how can we deal with anger correctly, especially when it can rise so quickly?

When Anger arises, we may not be able to control the feeling of Anger, but it is our choice whether we lash out from it. Some may choose to hold Anger in and let it fester and grow. Others may turn it into self-criticism, frustration, or hopelessness. This can be very hard with mental illness.

As I am writing this today, I had a bout of Anger, and I frightened my family. I didn't sin, but I certainly should have handled my conduct better. I am called to be their protector, but sometimes I behave like an oppressor.

There are days when I start to see a glimmer of "earthly hope" that the rough seas are behind me, and then suddenly, BOOM! Anger appears out of nowhere.

"Therefore, to him who thinks he stands watch out that he does not fall" (1 Corinthians 10:12). As long as I am alive in this earthen vessel, anger will be mine to wrestle with. And no man can wrestle it for me.

And that is good news.

Anger is not my enemy; it is a messenger. Mastered Anger can become clarity, but if we let it lead instead of inform, it will take us places wisdom would never choose. Anger is fast because it is designed for survival, but wisdom is slow because it is designed for direction.

How can a person grab Anger before it jumps out? What would it look like to pause and let God into that first moment? What does that mean when considering the topic of mental illness?

"A man without control of his Anger is like a city left without walls and broken into" (Proverbs 25:28 ESV). A city with no protection is overrun by the enemy. When we don't guard ourselves and turn away Anger (Proverbs 29:8), our enemy, Satan, comes in and takes over. He sets up his throne in our hearts and minds, and we are then blinded to the truth.

Ask yourself: Is it possible to mistake emotional intensity for truth?

"Where there is no vision, the people perish" (Proverbs 29:18 KJV).

For us to combat Anger, we have to see it for what it is. Anger is often a secondary emotion, and it is usually triggered by a perceived threat, injustice or unfairness, violation of expectations or boundaries, or fear, such as loss of control, respect, love, or certainty.

We need to be "quick to hear" and "slow to get angry" (James 1:19). So when Anger surfaces, we need to listen for the root cause. As we learn to discern, we begin training ourselves to become more aware of what is happening around us and within us (1 Corinthians 2:14). Much like an experienced boxer, we can start to see what the opponent is going to hit with next, and we can dodge or jab in response. Spiritually speaking, of course. Do not start throwing fists.

As we learn to exercise self-control, we learn to fight and box in such a way that we are not merely hitting the air (1 Corinthians 9:26).

There is Anger according to what God says is wrong (Isaiah 5:25), which is healthy Anger. But when we use self-righteous Anger, or unhealthy Anger, we are not doing God's will (James 1:20). That Anger may feel very real to us, and we may have an explanation for it, but that does not mean it is correct (Luke 16:14–15) or that we are expressing it in a wholesome manner (Proverbs 29:22).

In your Anger are you trying to justify yourself or God (Job 32:2)? Whose methods are you using (James 3:11, 13)?

Michael, the archangel of God, when disputing with the devil about Moses' body, did not hurl insults, mock, or use abusive language (Jude 9). He was humble, submitted himself to God's authority, resisted the devil (James 4:7), and allowed judgment and penalty to remain in the Father's hands (Psalm 62:11).

What is the reason for your Anger? What ignites that emotion within you? What do you SEE occurring in your life? What do you HEAR running through your thoughts?

We have to take those thoughts prisoner and hold them up to God's will. If you do let anger slip out, repent, make amends (Matthew 5:23–24), reevaluate, and examine why it surfaced in the first place (2 Corinthians 13:5).

James 4:1–2 tells us that quarrels and conflicts come when our inner desires are not met, and that some fall into sin while trying to satisfy them. Yet we don't have some things simply because we do not ask God for them.

For example, if you are angry because you do not feel respected by your wife, or because you don't feel loved by your husband, how do you handle it? Do you sin and go beyond God's will to try to force it? Or do you seek God Himself and ask Him to help supply your needs?

Not all fights and arguments are over sinful desires, but they can still lead to sin. Ask God to help you see and hear. Ask Him to help you understand the war going on within yourself between wants and needs, between right and wrong (Romans 7:15). Ask Him to search you and know your heart, to put you to the test and know your anxious thoughts, to see if there is anything harmful in you (Psalm 139:23–24). Implore Him to lead you down the correct path.

Between stimulus and response, there is a small space. When we learn to pause, that space gets a little bigger. Put God's will and words into that gap, and walk wisely.

Here is a simple framework to help evaluate and identify where your Anger is coming from: **A.N.G.E.R.**

A- Acknowledge. Name the emotion honestly. "I'm angry." We need to name it to tame it. These are signals, not to shame you, but to alert you.

N- Notice the source. What is actually threatened? Ego, comfort, control, justice?

G- Get perspective. What is true vs. what am I assuming? Engage the prefrontal cortex, slow down, and think.

E- Evaluate spiritually. Does this response reflect Christ? Is this righteous Anger or selfish Anger?

R- Respond, don't react. Choose a measured, intentional action.

The truth is that, much like anxiety and fear, if we let Anger grow, it can increase and get worse.

"Let all bitterness, anger, and wrath, shouting and slander be removed from you, along with malice" (Ephesians 4:31 CSB).

Uncontrolled Anger can lead to wrath. Wrath is intense, violent rage or vengeful fury. Historically and psychologically, it has been considered a temporary state of madness because a person is literally out of their "right mind." If Anger is allowed to go uncontrolled or is not dealt with correctly, a person may be tempted to shout or even speak ill of someone behind their back. All of this can become seed that grows into bitterness or even hatred (Hebrews 12:15).

"Whoever is angry with his brother without cause shall be in danger of the judgment" (Matthew 5:22 NKJV).

That is a serious penalty for Anger, isn't it? Considering the previous verse, Jesus associates anger with murder. Anger left uncontrolled can cause bitterness and self-seeking. Cain killed Abel because of this.

"Everyone who hates his brother or sister is a murderer and we know that no murderer has eternal life remaining in him" (1 John 3:15).

One who hates is considered a murderer in God's view because their heart is not right. Their walls have come down, and Satan has come in and set up rule. After all, he was a murderer from the beginning, and there is no truth in him (John 8:44). God tells us that those who are self-serving and don't follow the truth are actually obeying unrighteousness (Romans 2:8). When we operate from wicked intentions, we make ourselves enemies of God in our minds (Colossians 1:21).

Anger is a slippery slope if left unresolved.

So ask yourself: Where do I have anger that needs to be addressed? Have I allowed anger to grow into bitterness or even hatred?

Have you ever wondered how Joseph, after nearly being murdered, sold into slavery by his own brothers, lied about, falsely imprisoned, left, and seemingly forgotten, was not overcome with bitterness and hatred years later?

He had moved forward with God on his path. He chose, out of love, to serve God and his fellow humanity instead of becoming selfish. His brothers were terrified in his presence (Genesis 45:3), but he encouraged them not to worry or even be angry with themselves (verse 5).

By God's grace and loving guidance, Joseph realized that they meant evil toward him, but God used it for good and allowed him to go through those ordeals to preserve the lives of many people (Genesis 50:20). He didn't hold on to hatred and bitterness. Instead, he chose forgiveness while ultimately giving the matter over to God (Genesis 50:19).

Joseph may have been enslaved physically, but spiritually, he was set free by God's love and guiding hand.

Whom can you serve and help in the midst of your trials and hardships? How many lives do you impact for the greater good? Where are you a "slave" to resentment and need to be freed through forgiveness? Where can you be more like Christ and show compassion?

I have been overweight for most of my life and have tried many fad diets that promised to shed pounds with little to no effort. Just "eat this," or "drink that," or "take this supplement," or "count this," "carry the three and subtract the fiber..."

Does any of this sound familiar to you or someone you know?

Almost every time I did that, some weight would come off, but eventually it came back, usually with reinforcements. I had not put in the real discipline of learning new ways or developing habits that could sustain them. I was trying not to eat "bad stuff," but I had not replaced it with a working knowledge of what was truly good. I subtracted without adding, got the wrong answer, and was worse off in the end.

"When an unclean spirit has gone out of a person, it passes through waterless places seeking rest, and finding none, it says 'I will return to my house from which I came'" (Luke 11:24 ESV).

Do you wrestle with a "demon" of uncontrolled Anger? How long has that been going on? What happens when you finally get a good grasp on it, or when it seems to have left for a while?

"And when it comes, it finds the house swept and put in order. Then it goes and brings seven other spirits more evil than itself…" (Luke 11:25–26 ESV).

God doesn't just call us to avoid sinning. He doesn't want us to simply get rid of unhealthy anger. That void must be filled with something else, or the anger will return and most likely become worse.

We are called to put away all anger, wrath, slander, and all evil, selfish practices (Colossians 3:8–9). In their place, just like renovating an old home, we replace them with good and holy practices. We are to put on the new self, which is renewed in knowledge after the image of our Creator (Colossians 3:10).

"So, as those who have been chosen of God, holy and beloved, put on a heart of compassion, kindness, humility, gentleness, and patience; bearing with one another and forgiving one another, whoever has a complaint against anyone; just as the Lord forgave you, so must you do also" (Colossians 3:12-13). God isn't just giving us a list of dos and don'ts. He has given us a plan that can mold us into the image of Christ (Romans 8:29). He doesn't want us to use

His Word as a checklist, but as a transformational guide that gets absorbed into our minds and overflows into our lives.

He wants us to be like David and have a heart after His own heart (Acts 13:22). This includes doing God's will, but it goes much deeper than that. It reaches into our character, love, motivation, reverence, humility, and willingness to repent.

God does not see as we do. While we may see our failures, or the failures of others, and how anger creeps up and sometimes overcomes us, God sees our hearts (1 Samuel 16:7). He is not calling us to perfection alone. He is calling us to come out of the dark, to stand, and to follow Him. Being angry and not sinning is a process, not a destination. And as long as we are fighting this battle as soldiers of Christ (2 Timothy 2:3), we can be more than victorious, even in the face of mental illness.

"Be angry yet do not sin; on your bed search your heart and be still. Offer the sacrifices of the righteous and trust in the LORD" (Psalm 4:4–5 BSB).

Search your heart and listen for the root causes of your anger. I encourage you to trust in Him, His Word, and His might as you undertake this work. If we listen to our own thoughts and reasoning alone, we will get off track.

Pause before speaking, pray before confronting, and seek understanding before correcting. Our hearts can be very deceptive (Jeremiah 17:9); that is why we need to let God give us a new one (Ezekiel 36:26).

Chapter 9

The Past, Shame & Guilt

"I don't trust myself", that is what I told one counselor. Between my rapid mood swings and impulsive decision-making, I was a loose cannon in many areas of my life.

When I tried to sleep, my mind would ruminate and dwell on past experiences. Most of those memories involved situations where I felt uncomfortable, worried, or confused. Since my job was constantly changing, with layoffs, new job sites, and different people, there was always a heightened level of stress present.

The memories we most easily recall are often deeply imprinted, episodic, and highly emotional. They may include shocking "flashbulb" memories, milestones of personal significance, or traumatic events. Since I have a mental illness, I experienced intense, rapidly changing emotions that brought deeply engraved memories with them. Situations that may have seemed normal to someone else could bring abject terror into my mind.

I would often recall horrible things I had done in anger, fear, or frustration. My family had suffered because of my words and actions, when I should have been their protector and role model. I was a vessel full of thoughts and emotions on a wild and rough sea of mental storms.

How do you handle and process regrets? What do you do with the memories of wrongs you have committed? When we see how we may have negatively impacted loved ones in our lives, how can we move forward?

"It is a trustworthy statement, worthy of full acceptance, Christ Jesus came into the world to save sinners, of whom I am the worst" (1 Timothy 1:15 BSB).

Paul had persecuted the church and had even consented to some being put to death (Acts 22:4; 8:1). He would enter houses, drag men and women away, and put them into prison. He had many things in his past to regret. So how did he handle it and move forward?

Notice that he did not try to hide it or sweep it under the rug. He admitted that he was guilty. If you are going to make forward progress, you must own and take responsibility for your past (1 John 1:8–9). Paul knew where he had been, and you know where you have been. Jesus knows too, and He came to save us. That includes saving us from ourselves (Ephesians 4:22).

The example of God's patience with Paul should give us hope and comfort because He offers the same to us. Do you offer yourself patience and forgiveness, or do you condemn and beat yourself up over the past? What do you dwell on and tell yourself often? Are you currently processing life through old "programming"? How do you know?

"Now as he was traveling, it happened that he was approaching Damascus, and suddenly a light from heaven flashed around him; and he fell to the ground and heard a voice saying to him, 'Saul, Saul, why are you persecuting me?'" (Acts 9:3–4).

How can we allow God's light to shine into our darkened hearts and minds and reveal where we may be hiding? Where should you be moving forward with Him toward His calling?

Saul got up from the ground, and though his eyes were open, he could see nothing (verse 8). What does it take for our eyes to be opened? What would it take for you to see where you are truly blind?

Saul thought he was doing the right things the whole time, but he was far off course (Acts 23:1). Like Elijah, God gave Saul, later Paul, instructions to travel on. God also sent a messenger to give him more knowledge (Acts 9:10ff).

If you find an area where you are blind, are you willing to see the truth and take action? Where do you need to travel farther down the path? Where do you need more instruction and knowledge? Should you seek God in prayer, speak with an elder, or perhaps meet with a counselor to gain a better perspective?

So how did Paul keep his mind clear from the haunting thoughts of past failures?

"Forgetting what lies behind and reaching forward to what lies ahead, I press on toward the goal" (Philippians 3:13–14). Paul was not ignorant of his past, but he did not let it keep him from reaching for his future. The idea here is to neglect those thoughts. He didn't feed them, mull over them, or repeat them again and again in his mind. He focused on moving ahead.

How many times do you get stuck worrying about what you have done, said, or thought in a past situation? Do those concerns take over your mind and focus?

Consider what would happen if you tried to steer your car by looking only in the rearview mirror. That would be foolish, right? It wouldn't be long before you crashed. But how many of us try to drive our lives the same way, letting the past dictate our forward direction?

Paul knew the past, but he chose to reach forward toward God's calling and the future.

Do you know the difference between shame and guilt?

Guilt says, *"I made a mistake,"* while Shame says, *"I am the mistake."* Shame is more than embarrassment. Embarrassment is behavior-focused, external, and momentary. Shame is internal, identity-focused, and enduring. Shame can include hiding, shrinking, covering, pretending, or even overcompensating. It can consume us when our identity is attached to failure instead of growth.

Paul knew he had made grievous errors in the past, but those errors were not his identity. He knew that his value and worth were assigned by God through Christ, not by his history (Philippians 3:3–7). He knew he was guilty and even admitted it, but he also knew that as long as he moved forward in Christ, he was not a failure. Paul refused to succumb to shame.

Adam was overcome with shame when his identity and relationship with God changed, but he didn't take responsibility for himself or his actions.

Do you have shame or guilt? Maybe both? What is a healthy way to move forward knowing that?

You may have made many mistakes in the past, but those mistakes are not your identity. If you struggle with a mental illness, you are not your disorder. God seeks us out to reconcile us, clothe us, and lift us back up.

"Those who look to Him are radiant, and their faces shall never be ashamed" (Psalm 34:5 ESV). Shame can be a good indicator of who truly reigns within your heart and mind. Paul said that he was "not ashamed" of the good news about Jesus (Romans 1:16), and that was because Christ ruled within him (Galatians 2:20).

Who rules within your heart and mind? We can see what governs within by what is produced without (Matthew 7:16). What do your thoughts, words, and actions show? Not just the outcomes connected to struggling with mental illness, but the harvest of what you are intentionally planting. The pursuits and focus that fill your days matter. Wisdom is vindicated by her children (Luke 7:35).

Take heart. You are a living, breathing human being whom God loves and calls to know Him and His care more deeply.

The Bible has many verses on forgiveness, but you would be hard-pressed to find one on "self-forgiveness." In the Sermon on the Mount, Jesus said that we are to forgive others their trespasses, and if we don't, then God will not forgive us (Matthew 6:14–15). Doesn't it make sense, then, that we should forgive ourselves?

Ultimately, ALL sin is against God (Psalm 51:4). Paul knew he was forgiven by God. And if God forgave him, why should he not forgive himself? If we refuse to forgive ourselves, are we claiming to be more righteous or superior in judgment than God? Should we beat ourselves up and be mentally tortured by old mistakes?

For illustration, when something happens, such as failure, a missed opportunity, or letting someone down, two arrows can be fired at you. The first one strikes you, and it hurts. This comes from the event or circumstance, and it is painful. But the second arrow is the one you fire at yourself. That arrow is a choice.

That second arrow is what we tell ourselves about an event. It is what we keep going over and over again in our minds, and that is where suffering often comes from. Do you need to forgive yourself? Are you torturing yourself by going over past mistakes?

Biblical forgiveness is not shallow or sentimental. It is rooted in the depth, cost, and clarity of how God deals with sin. He doesn't excuse sin or pretend it didn't happen. He confronts it fully.

Forgiveness is not denial or pretending no wrong occurred. Forgiveness always absorbs a cost. Someone pays. In God's case, He bore it Himself. Forgiveness is not based on the offender's worthiness, but on God's character.

"Remember no more" does not mean God has amnesia. It means He does not hold it against us judicially. When we forgive ourselves, it does not validate the behavior; it calls us out of it. It releases vengeance (Romans 12:19), chooses not to hold the offense over ourselves or others (1 Corinthians 13:5), and entrusts justice to God.

When we forgive, we are not calling evil good (Isaiah 5:20). We are giving it to God, receiving His grace and mercy, and letting go of the frustration and bitterness we may hold against ourselves (Ephesians 4:31–32). Forgiveness removes emotional poison.

Ask yourself: Do I release the desire for "revenge" against myself, or do I still want suffering? Am I confusing forgiveness with emotional numbness or avoidance? Am I grounding my response in God's character, or in fear and anger?

Own your past. Ask forgiveness from those you have wronged (James 5:16; Matthew 5:23–24). Ask God to forgive you (Acts 8:22). Forgive yourself, and go forward and sin no more (John 8:11).

Don't let pride keep you stuck in shame (Proverbs 11:2). Be humble and move forward with wisdom. Keep in mind that as you work on taking a new path, others may not initially be supportive or feel at ease in your presence (Acts 9:26). Seeing is believing for many, and old patterns are hard to overcome. Trust is built through repentance, consistency, and time (Matthew 3:8).

This is a journey and a process that must be pursued day by day in your walk with God. There will be times when you slip up.

And that is okay.

God will still love you, and He will still call you onward (1 John 1:7–10).

For many years, I would become interested in a topic, buy a book about it, and then let it collect dust on a shelf. I have many "shelf help" books.

I eventually realized that getting excited and buying a book was not the same as reading it and truly understanding it. Association with something is not the same as transformation. Many scholars possess deep, expert knowledge of the Bible, but they are not Christians.

As human beings, we often assume change happens when someone receives enough information, good advice, or logical arguments. We have discussed many topics throughout this book, but that does not mean they will affect anyone's life or help someone walk with a mental illness. It is a choice whether we apply the knowledge or not.

This is also true regarding shame and guilt. They may temporarily cause us to feel pressure, but if they are not handled correctly, we may try to avoid those signals. People rarely change simply because they were told the truth. They change when the conditions of the heart, mind, and environment align. Understanding this helps explain why some people transform dramatically while others remain stuck for decades.

The following framework can help you understand what actually causes change. Change typically occurs when several forces converge.

Awareness: seeing reality clearly.
Change begins when a person clearly recognizes a problem. But awareness is not merely intellectual knowledge. Many people know something is wrong but have not emotionally accepted it. True awareness occurs when you can no longer deny the reality of your situation, much like the prodigal son, who "came to his senses" (Luke 15:17).

Ask yourself: Am I clearly seeing my situation, or am I minimizing it? What evidence am I ignoring? What patterns keep repeating in my life?

Ownership: accepting responsibility.
Change cannot begin while blame is being placed elsewhere. Ownership means that while circumstances, mental illness, anger, or shame may influence us, our actions are still our responsibility. Otherwise, it is just like in the garden. Instead of taking responsibility, we try to redirect the blame.

Ask yourself: What parts of my situation are actually under my control? Where am I blaming others instead of taking action? If nothing changes, what responsibility do I bear for that outcome?

Discomfort: when pain becomes greater than comfort.
Most people do not change while their current behavior still provides enough comfort. Many people are more comfortable with familiar problems than unfamiliar solutions. Change occurs when the pain of remaining the same becomes greater than the pain of changing. This can happen through health scares, relationship consequences, financial pressure, spiritual conviction, or accumulated regret.

"No discipline seems enjoyable at the time, but it is painful. Later on, however, it yields a harvest of righteousness" (Hebrews 12:11 BSB).

Ask yourself: What is the long-term cost of continuing my current habits? What future am I choosing by avoiding discipline today? What would my life look like in five years if nothing changed?

Vision: a clear picture of a better future.
People rarely endure hardship without a meaningful vision. Vision creates motivation, and without it, discipline feels pointless. "Without vision, the people perish" (Proverbs 29:18).

Ask yourself: What kind of person do I want to become? What kind of life would make present sacrifices worthwhile? What legacy do I want to leave behind?

Capability: believing change is possible.
If you believe change is impossible, you will not make the effort. Repeated failure often destroys belief in personal capability.

Encouragement and small wins rebuild that belief. Do you believe that you can do greater things through Christ's power (Philippians 4:13)?

Ask yourself: Do I believe change is actually possible for me? What small step could prove that change is possible? Where have I succeeded before that I may be forgetting?

<u>**Support:**</u> environment and relationships.
Human behavior is strongly influenced by the environment. People surrounded by supportive relationships and healthy expectations change far more easily than those who are isolated in unhealthy environments. Sit at the table with warriors, and the conversation is different. If you surround yourself with complainers and negativity, you will be encouraged to do the same. Find those who will fight alongside you and support your forward movement.

"Two are better than one because if either of them falls, one can help the other up" (Ecclesiastes 4:9–10).

Ask yourself: Do the people around me support my growth or reinforce my weaknesses? What environments make my good habits easier? What environments sabotage my discipline?

<u>**Consistency:**</u> small actions repeated.
Consistency beats intensity every time. Jim Rohn said, *"Success is a few good habits repeated daily, and failure is a few bad habits repeated daily."* Change rarely comes from dramatic moments. It usually comes from repeated small decisions. When we can be trusted with the little things, we can do more (Luke 16:10). This takes discipline, which, in

its simplest form, is being able to give yourself a command and follow it.

Ask yourself: What small habit, repeated daily, would change my life over time? Am I waiting for motivation instead of practicing consistency? Am I willing to be disciplined?

Information by itself, knowledge without action, other people's expectations, and so much more do not truly bring lasting change. Emotional moments can inspire movement, but habits sustain transformation.

Don't let the feeling of being alone, mental illness, anxiety, depression, hopelessness, fear, anger, guilt, or shame keep you from moving forward toward your future and overcoming by God's Spirit. It won't truly happen by your understanding and strength alone. Be the person God has designed you to be, calls you to become, and gives you the power to reach for. *"Don't be deceived, God is not mocked; for whatever a man sows, that he will also reap"* (Galatians 6:7 NKJV).

What seeds are you planting in your mind, in your heart, and in your life? What are you nurturing and feeding? Are you trusting God to help them grow and flourish (1 Corinthians 3:6)?

The beautiful thing about a seed is that it produces much more than was planted. If you plant one kernel of corn, you can reap many ears of corn from it. Planting and nurturing the seed of a small daily habit may seem insignificant at first, but in the long run, it can reap many blessings for you and for others.

Did you know that the inventor of the Ferris wheel never met the inventor of the merry-go-round? They traveled in different circles.

It is my honor and privilege to be traveling in your circle as you read and follow along with me in this book. It is my hope and aim that, in some small way, I may encourage you along your journey.

I recently became a grandpa, and my grandson is at the age where he is starting to put his shoes on by himself. Now, if you take a look at your shoes, you'll see the concave arc in the middle and the big toes pointing forward beside each other. Have you ever seen a little kid wearing shoes with the big toes pointing in opposite directions? Let me ask you: Do they have their shoes on the wrong feet? And if they are the wrong feet, whose feet are they? Or maybe they have their feet in the wrong shoes.

Four hundred pounds and three years ago, I woke up and realized I had been wearing the "wrong shoes" for most of my life. Some people wake up at twenty, thirty, or forty, and some never wake up. I was coming up on forty-nine years of age. My dad had passed away at forty-nine. My health was deplorable, my finances were out of control, and my family life was chaotic at best.

Then one day it hit me: *This is not a dress rehearsal. I only get one go-around on this planet.*

I had grown older, but I had stopped growing personally.

So I did a lot of soul-searching, praying, and research. I started listening to Jim Rohn, Earl Nightingale, and Charlie "Tremendous"

Jones. I began reading more, and one day I came across a John Maxwell book.

And I started growing again.

Along my journey, I also took up running, and from that, I learned a priceless lesson: the hard part is not getting to the finish line of a race. The hard part is getting to the starting line.

I want to encourage you to remember the miles, feet, and inches you have already put in on your journey to get where you are right now. Sometimes we need to look behind us to see how far we've come (1 Corinthians 6:11). And I want to cheer you on as you step toward new starting lines, wear the "right shoes," and reach for the best version of yourself that you were designed to become. It is in movement that better is found. "Let's rid ourselves of every obstacle and the sin which so easily entangles us, and let's run with endurance the race that is set before us" (Hebrews 12:1).

Chapter 10

Real Healing

"Why doesn't God just heal me?" I have often struggled with that question. Jesus went about healing people in the first century. Why not me? Why not now?

In hindsight, I see that God has answered that question. "I consider that the sufferings of this present time are not comparable to the glory about to be revealed in us" (Romans 8:18 BLB). I can be "pressured in every way but not crushed, even perplexed but not driven to despair" (2 Corinthians 4:8 AB), because I know that my "momentary burden" is preparing me for eternal glory (2 Corinthians 4:17).

God says that all of creation is subject to the curse (Romans 8:20), and that is a good thing because there is hope in the end (2 Peter 3:13). This world is broken, and we live among broken people while leading our own broken lives. The answer is not found in this world.

He reigns in heaven at the right hand of God (Acts 2:33), and He is in the process of reconciling the world to Himself (2 Corinthians 5:19). I am fully confident that His arm is not too short to reach me, and He is not deaf to my prayers (Isaiah 59:1). He has begun a good work in me and will see it through to completion (Philippians 1:6). In His hands, the end of my story is so much better than the beginning (Ecclesiastes 7:8).

"Have you not known? Have you not heard? The everlasting God, the LORD, the Creator of the ends of the earth, never faints nor is weary. His understanding is unsearchable. He gives power to the weak, and those who have no might He increases strength" (Isaiah 40:28–29 NKJV).

And what do I have that I did not receive from God (1 Corinthians 4:7)? All things were created for Him and through Him. He is before everything, and in Him all things are held together (Colossians 1:17). As I humbly examine all of that, I am overwhelmed and in awe that He knows me so well that the very hairs on my head are numbered (Luke 12:7).

Who am I that God should care so deeply and show so much attention to me (Psalm 8:4)? Should I not accept both the good and the difficult things He allows into my life (Job 2:10)? Who am I to argue with God and claim that He doesn't know what He is doing (Romans 9:20), as though He has made a mistake by allowing me, or a loved one, to have a mental illness?

Doesn't He have the right, as the Creator (Romans 9:21), to mold my earthen vessel (2 Corinthians 4:7)? Am I to complain and question God's wisdom and character from my lack of them (Philippians 2:14–15)?

No. He tells me that even in this weak form, His might can be shown (2 Corinthians 12:9), and that within me, His light can clear the darkness in my heart and understanding (2 Corinthians 4:6).

As a parent, I don't prepare the road for my children; I prepare my children for the road. My Heavenly Father is doing the same for me. And seeing that the road He calls me to climb is difficult and goes upward (Matthew 7:13–14), along a narrow mountain path (Hebrews 12:22), I will gladly endure hardship and discipline (Hebrews 12:7) because I am His loved and precious child (1 John 5:2).

Therefore, I will keep asking Him for wisdom (James 1:5), and He will give it (Luke 11:9; 1 John 3:22). I will keep seeking, and He will help me find (Luke 11:9). I will keep knocking, and the door will be opened to me (Matthew 7:8).

He is a good Father and knows how to give good things to those who ask (Matthew 7:11), pure and perfect gifts (James 1:17). Seeing such great love (John 3:16), I will seek to HEAR and understand His voice (Matthew 7:26). I will strive to SEE His light (Ephesians 1:18), even when mental illness may darken my view. And I will work even harder to see through His vision (Matthew 6:22), because only then can I truly know that my mind is not blinded (2 Corinthians 4:4).

Have you ever thought about what it would be like if you, or a loved one, did not have a mental illness? And not just wanting to avoid the burden and struggles that come with it, or the thoughts, focus, emotions, and energy it consumes, but have you considered life without it? What would that actually look like or feel like?

Job said that if you are a human being, then your days will be short and full of trouble (Job 14:1). What other troubles would God allow into your life? What other troubles would we usher in if our attention were freed to wander even more (Ecclesiastes 10:15)?

If you gathered with every friend, family member, and acquaintance, and you all wrote down your biggest struggles in life and put them into a hat, would you want to keep your own, or would you dare to take someone else's? If everything were perfect here on earth, would we even look forward to heaven?

"When the devils have gone, can we get our old selves back?" **(Dragon Seed, Pearl S. Buck).** Is this the sentiment you hold? Do you believe that if your "demon" of mental illness were gone, you might get your old life back? Ask yourself: Is that my desire, or is it a God-inspired one?

It is not wrong to want to avoid difficulty. But at what cost do we, as human beings, try to avoid it? Struggles refine us and help strengthen our resolve (Zechariah 13:9). They reveal what is within our hearts and expose our integrity, or lack of it. We must decrease so that He may increase (John 3:30).

God calls us to put off the old man and put on a new way of life that is renewed in knowledge (Colossians 3:9–10). That passage speaks to sin, missing the mark of God's perfection (Romans 3:23), but it can also relate to our errant thought processes (2 Corinthians 10:5), with or without mental illness, as well as our attitudes and our reliance upon God.

As Christians, when we continue growing and maturing, our ways of thinking, reasoning, and speaking will change and focus more on applying His love in our lives (1 Corinthians 13:11). Our war may not be a physical one against flesh and blood (Ephesians 6:12), but we do wage war spiritually, and those who have gone off to fight do not come back the same.

Active combat can change one's personality, perspective, and even capacity to function in daily life. God calls us to oppose spiritual enemies and darkness, and when we are lit up with His might, we are **changed for the better**. We are given an eternal perspective, and our conversation turns toward higher things (Philippians 3:20).

We no longer see this world as we once did (Hebrews 11:13), because we have become spiritually discerning (1 Corinthians 2:14) and aware of the enemy's traps (2 Corinthians 2:11). By God's grace, we can see the great forces moving in and around us (Proverbs 22:11). We have gone from being people focused on the flesh to soldiers of Christ (2 Timothy 2:3–4).

While we may be aware of the past, He calls us to move forward into the future, today (Hebrews 3:15). But that may not always go the way we think or hope it should. For example, if a person is looking for an "easy" way to get in shape, they have already failed. That journey takes discipline, consistency, patience, perseverance, and even some setbacks. The same is true spiritually, for we must go through many trials to enter the kingdom of God (Acts 14:22).

Some of those trials may involve the discipline, not punishment, but refinement, of a mental illness allowed into your life (Hebrews 12:7). And just like in Job's time, Satan may be trying to use evil against us, but God can use it for good (2 Corinthians 12:7ff).

When we endure significant hardships, they can culminate in spiritual endurance, growth, and victory. They test our faith to see if it is real and viable. They show what we truly believe and where we place our trust, and that allows us to learn patience (James 1:3). If we let that patience do its work, then we can thrive and mature as Christians, hold deeply to faith, hope, and love, and walk wisely with a pure heart. "Whoever strives to save his life will lose it, and whoever loses his life will preserve it" (Luke 17:33).

We are to take up our cross daily (Luke 9:23), follow Jesus' thinking, teachings, and example, and walk in the power of the Holy Spirit (1 Thessalonians 1:5), even in the middle of our rough seas. This requires actively putting to death the reasoning and desires that go against His will, and that is no small undertaking (Galatians 5:24). This will be a lifelong war, but take heart: we are not left alone in this endeavor (Deuteronomy 31:6).

"But this is not fair."

Have you ever had that thought? If you have, you are correct. It is not fair that there should be so much sickness and death in life. That was not God's intention or design (Romans 5:12). But in His loving wisdom, before the earth was even created (Revelation 13:8), He made provision for them. And when the time was right (Galatians 4:4), He sent His Son to pay the price for sin (2 Corinthians 5:21).

Was it fair for Jesus to die for your errors? For mine? Absolutely not. But because of His love for His Father and for us, He chose to do it anyway (Hebrews 12:2).

If we consider our mental illness from an eternal perspective, we are far more blessed than we realize and can have joy that outlasts physical trouble (Isaiah 41:10). It is not fair at all that we can face the thought of sickness and even death without being afraid. Indeed, God has given us an "unfair advantage" over the enemy (1 Corinthians 15:26).

We can be uplifted and encouraged like the apostle Paul and confidently say, "O Death, where is your sting? O Hades, where is your victory?" (1 Corinthians 15:55 NKJV), because thanks be to God, He gives us victory through Jesus Christ (verse 57).

Jesus is greater than Satan and has disarmed and defeated him (Colossians 2:15). When we are filled with Christ, we can truly overcome this world (1 John 4:4). That doesn't mean your mental illness will instantly be healed, or healed at all, but it does mean you can have assurance that whatever is thrown at you, you can be more than victorious (1 Corinthians 15:57).

Once you have learned to take your thoughts prisoner, punch holes in the darkness with light, seek purpose in God's might, challenge anxiety, see hope, drive out fear, wrestle with anger, deal with the past, and move beyond shame and guilt, will you not be in a better place? Mentally? Spiritually? Relationally?

This is the road He calls us to follow, and it will be messy and not always linear.

I remember one of the times I was very low and had an announcement made after the church service. *"I didn't feel like living,"* was the message. Brethren may not always understand or know how to respond effectively in those situations.

Have you ever felt that "church" is only for perfect people? Everyone has struggles and thoughts that may be difficult to get a handle on, but how many of those struggles are shared with others? Do you actively ask for help from brethren? If you don't, does that come from shame or fear?

James 5:14 tells us that if any are sick, the elders should pray over them. Does this not also include mental illness?

There were many times over the years when I did not want to be alive. I felt like Solomon, who spoke of the "difficult days" that come and the years when you say, "I have no pleasure in them" (Ecclesiastes 12:1). I remembered my Creator in those days, and I had hope in the middle of no hope. It was a God-given hope that carried me through, knowing that I had a home waiting for me in eternity (John 14:2). I knew that my weak body of flesh would be raised a spiritual body full of power and glory (1 Corinthians 15:43), and that I was a coheir (Romans 8:17) with the King of Kings and Lord of Lords (Revelation 19:16). That was truly comforting knowledge.

What would you do if everything you hoped for and dreamed of came true? God delivered the Israelites from slavery in Egypt and had warned them of this very thing:

"When you eat and are satisfied, and you build good houses and live in them, and when your herds and flocks increase, and your silver and gold increase, and everything that you have increases" (Deuteronomy 8:12–13).

It would be great if the text continued, "Then you will be thankful and praise God and follow Him faithfully." But that is not the warning He gives. No. He says, *"Then your heart will become proud, and you will forget the LORD your God"* (verse 14).

What happens if you are freed from the bondage of mental illness? Whom WILL you serve (Joshua 24:15)? Whom DO you serve today? God or your own desires? Do you seek God to see His face (Psalm 27:8), know Him (Jeremiah 22:16), and be known by Him (Galatians 4:9), or do you seek only His hands (John 12:37), as if He were a genie who grants wishes?

"What does it profit a man to gain the whole world and forfeit his soul?" (Mark 8:36 ESV).

In the past, I wondered why Jesus healed people in New Testament times, yet I had not received healing today. God allowed me time to understand. Jesus' healings were physical miracles, and they showed that He was indeed sent from God above (Hebrews 2:4). But that was not the true, lasting, eternal focus of Jesus' ministry. He was the Great Physician (Mark 2:17), and His mission was to seek and save the lost (Luke 19:10).

"Which is easier, to say, 'Your sins be forgiven you,' or to say, 'Rise and walk?' But that you may know that the Son of Man has authority on earth to forgive sins," He said to the man with paralysis, "I say to you, rise, pick up your bed and go home" (Luke 5:23–24 NKJV).

And the man got up and went home glorifying God (verse 25). When the people saw it, they were amazed, glorified God, and were filled with fear (verse 26).

Jesus *physically* mended people to show the deeper truth that He could *spiritually* restore people. The real healing we need is spiritual. Jesus said, "It is not the healthy who need a doctor, but the sick. I have not come to call the righteous, but sinners" (Mark 2:17 BLB).

All sin and deserve eternal death (Romans 6:23), but even some who believe they are well may not be. Many are weak and sick, and some are even sleeping (1 Corinthians 11:30), because they do not truly examine themselves and their walk with God (2 Corinthians 13:5).

Ask yourself, "How am I doing spiritually?"

That answer should not take very long, but it should not be automatic either. A truthful answer usually lives in the space between immediate awareness and honest reflection. If you answered instantly, there is a risk you may be giving a default, socially acceptable response. If it takes too long, it may mean you are not regularly checking in with your inner man. Or you may have a mood disorder and not "feel" secure about your answer.

No matter what your answer is, what does God say about your spiritual well-being? Go beyond your own perception. What does God's perspective tell you?

It is only **in Christ** that all spiritual blessings can be found (Ephesians 1:3). True joy, love, and peace are fruit of the Spirit that this world can never provide (Galatians 5:22). The world offers the lust of the flesh, the lust of the eyes, and the pride of life (1 John 2:16), but those are temporary pursuits that bring no lasting fulfillment because they all pass away in the end (1 John 2:17).

So ask yourself: Am I in Christ? How do I know? How can I know? This goes beyond a subjective feeling, because God says it can be objectively true. If we run ahead and don't abide in the teachings of Christ, then we will be lost (2 John 1:9).

It is only through Christ, the one and only mediator between God and man (1 Timothy 2:5), that we can have reconciliation (2 Corinthians 5:19). It is only through Christ that one can come to the Father (1 John 2:23). If you do not have Jesus the Christ, you do not have access to the Father (Matthew 10:33).

Jesus is the prophet of God (Matthew 21:11). A prophet tells God's words to the people (Hebrews 1:1–2). Jesus is the High Priest (Hebrews 4:14–16). A high priest mediated between man and God.

He could go into the Most Holy Place, behind the veil, into God's presence and make atonement for the people's sins (Leviticus 16:14–15).

Jesus died upon the cross (Hebrews 9:26, 28) as God's sacrificial Lamb (John 1:29) to take away sin and usher in the New Testament (Hebrews 9:15). He was raised three days later. He defeated death (1 Corinthians 15:4) and later ascended back to heaven (Acts 1:9–11).

Jesus is the now-reigning King (Luke 1:32–33). His kingdom is a spiritual one (John 18:36), and He is the door that provides entrance (John 10:9). Those who enter and remain within will be saved (Revelation 2:10).

Without Jesus, a person is spiritually dead in sin (Romans 6:23), with no eternal home waiting in heaven, only torment (Matthew 25:46). Jesus offers eternal salvation. This isn't about self-improvement or overcoming mental illness. This is about spiritual rescue and restoration.

If you are in Christ, then you can receive all His spiritual blessings. You are forgiven (1 John 2:12), spiritually regenerated (Titus 3:5), made new (2 Corinthians 5:17), adopted into His family (Ephesians 1:5), and sealed by the Holy Spirit (Ephesians 1:13), who is the guarantee of our heavenly inheritance (1 Peter 1:3).

It is not just believing things about Jesus, but being **United with Him** and His might. God initiates through grace, Jesus' sacrifice, and calling (2 Thessalonians 2:14). Man responds by faith (Romans 10:17), repentance (Acts 3:19), and obedience (Matthew 7:21). We don't earn salvation, but it is not passive either. We work alongside God, and through access to His might and grace, we overcome (Philippians 2:12).

I remember wanting to become a Christian as a young boy. The reason? I wanted to eat the bread and drink the juice from those cool little plastic cups. So I went to the front pew, confessed Christ, and was dunked under water.

Then, a week or so later, I was dunked again because I realized I had not done it for the right reason. Later, at twenty-five years of age, I truly understood and saw my need for Christ's atoning blood in my life. I obeyed God's commands from the heart (Romans 6:17).

Are you trusting in Jesus, or are you just agreeing with facts about Him? Have you actually turned from sin, or have you only felt bad about it (2 Corinthians 7:10)? Have you entered Christ, or are you standing outside observing?

If you have faith (John 3:16), repent (Acts 3:19), confess that Jesus is the Christ, the Son of the living God (Acts 8:37), and are baptized **into Christ** (Galatians 3:27), then you are trusting in Him and His finished work of salvation (Ephesians 2:8–9).

The Scriptures show a clear pattern of response and the process of turning to God. God's plan is not only to forgive you, but also to place you into Christ, where your identity, life, and future are completely changed. There, you can truly know that you belong to Him, based on His promises and the evidence of a transformed life.

Have you answered God's calling? Is there evidence of new life in you?

"Listen, now is God's acceptable time. Now is the day of salvation" (2 Corinthians 6:2 GWT).

"And now why are you waiting? Arise and be baptized, and wash away your sins, calling on the name of the Lord" (Acts 22:16 NKJV).

About The Author

Hello, my name is Daniel L. Thomason. I live in Northwest Indiana with my beautiful wife of thirty years, Elizabeth; my loving daughter, Morgan; and our two pups, Harmony and Daisy. Our oldest daughter, Alexxus, lives in Fishers, Indiana, with our son-in-law, Josh, and our grandson, Benjamin.

I have been blessed to be part of the Lord's body for many years and have had the pleasure of teaching and preaching, both locally and around the country. I originally wrote this book during a time when I was in the middle of many rough mental storms. God has blessed me with the opportunity to return to it later, with a better grasp of His perspective, and finish this work.

This is a labor of love born from my own personal struggles, including those I have inflicted upon my family. My hope is that my mess may become a message of comfort for those who are in the same, or a similar, boat. I hope and pray that you, or a loved one, may find encouragement and well-being as you examine God's message for your life, and that He may shine into your understanding and "light up" your vision.

"Lord, to whom shall we go? You have the words of eternal life." (John 6:68 NKJV*).*

"Your word is a lamp to my feet and a light to my path" (Psalm 119:105 NKJV*).*

You may see inner storms on the horizon (Matthew 16:3), but God can "calm them to a whisper" and "still the waves" (Psalm 107:29). Mental illness may toss us back and forth. We may even lose faith (James 1:6) and wonder if anything good can come from our situation (Psalm 119:68). But it is only in being anchored (Hebrews 6:19) to the Rock, Christ (1 Corinthians 10:4), who is "the same yesterday, today, and forever" (Hebrews 13:8), that we can truly be secured. May the Lord bless you and keep you as you travel through your life with Him.

www.ingramcontent.com/pod-product-compliance
Lightning Source LLC
LaVergne TN
LVHW100325210926
848480LV00003B/1259
* 9 7 9 8 2 3 4 1 1 2 3 9 2 *